SAYULITA
TRAVEL GUIDE
2024

Embark on a Magical Voyage
Through Mexico's Most
Enchanting Coastal Town

Marilyn Bell

Copyright © 2024, Marilyn Bell

All rights reserved.

TABLE OF CONTENTS

Introduction to Sayulita

Sayulita, Mexico – the energetic waterfront town that won my love from the second I showed up. Allow me to take you on an excursion through this beguiling heaven that enthrals explorers with its easygoing energy, vivid roads, and stunning sea shores.

Settled on the Pacific shoreline of Mexico, Sayulita is a little yet clamouring town in the province of Nayarit, only north of Puerto Vallarta. When you drop by Sayulita, you're wrapped by a feeling of warmth and unwinding that penetrates the air. The town's bohemian climate, combined with its regular magnificence, makes it a shelter for surfers, yogis, and nonconformists.

One of the primary things you'll see about Sayulita is its dynamic roads enhanced with beautiful wall paintings, varied shops, and interesting bistros. Meandering through the cobblestone roads, you'll experience a kaleidoscope of sights and sounds – from neighbourhood craftsmans offering their products to road entertainers entertaining bystanders. Each corner appears to have its own story to tell, and I ended up losing all sense of direction in the appeal, all things considered,

Something that attracted me to Sayulita is its standing as a riding mecca. With its reliable waves and warm waters, it's no big surprise that surfers from around the world run to its shores. Whether you're an old pro or a novice hoping to get your most memorable wave, Sayulita offers something for everybody. I spent endless hours out on the water, feeling the surge of adrenaline as I rode the waves underneath the brilliant sun.

Be that as it may, Sayulita isn't just about surfing - it's likewise a heaven for foodies. The town is overflowing with delectable restaurants presenting everything from conventional Mexican food to worldwide passage. One of my number one activities was investigating the neighbourhood taco stands, where I enjoyed a variety of delightful tacos overflowing with new fixings. What's more, we should not disregard the invigorating margaritas -

there's nothing very like tasting on a chilly margarita as you watch the nightfall over the sea.

Obviously, no outing to Sayulita would be finished without a visit to its immaculate sea shores. The primary oceanside, Playa Sayulita, is a vivacious centre point of movement, where you'll find sunbathers absorbing the beams, families building sandcastles, and merchants offering all that from new organic products to hand tailored makes. For a more separated encounter, you can venture to adjoining sea shores like Playa Los Muertos or Playa Carricitos, where you can loosen up in the serenity of nature.

Past its seashores and surf, Sayulita is additionally known for its dynamic social scene. Over time, the town plays host to different celebrations and occasions commending everything from music and dance to food and craftsmanship. One of the features of my excursion was going to the Day of the Dead festivals, where the roads woke up with vivid raised areas, elaborate outfits, and exuberant parades regarding the spirits of the left.

However much I adored investigating Sayulita's enthusiastic roads and unblemished sea shores, a portion of my most treasured recollections are of individuals I met en route. Local people, known as Sayuleros, are the absolute most amiable and most inviting individuals you'll at any point meet. From sharing stories over a feast to moving the night away at an ocean side huge fire, I felt a feeling of brotherhood and association that encouraged me at home.

In Sayulita, time appears to dial back, permitting you to drench yourself right now and appreciate the straightforward delights of life really. Whether you're relaxing on the oceanfront, investigating the town's unlikely treasures, or basically taking in the dusk with a virus drink close by, Sayulita has an approach to catching your heart and leaving you yearning for more.

So assuming you're desiring a departure from the rushing about of daily existence, I can't suggest Sayulita enough. Whether you're looking for experience, unwinding, or essentially a difference in pace, this beguiling Mexican town has something for everybody. Trust me, when you experience the sorcery of Sayulita, you won't ever need to leave.

Welcome to Sayulita

Welcome to Sayulita - a cut of heaven settled on the Pacific shore of Mexico, where lively culture, dazzling sea shores, and easygoing energies crash to make an extraordinary encounter. As somebody who has invested energy investigating every aspect of this enchanting town, let me be your aide as we set out on an excursion through the sights, sounds, and kinds of Sayulita.

Priorities straight - we should discuss energy. Sayulita has this mystical quality that immediately reassures you. From the second you show up, you can feel the burdens of regular day to day existence dissolve away as you're wrapped by a feeling of unwinding and peacefulness. The speed of life here is slow and sluggish, permitting you to really absorb the excellence of your environmental elements and embrace the laid-back way of life that characterises Sayulita.

Presently, we should discuss the sea shores - on the grounds that can we just be real, attracted you here the primary spot, correct? Sayulita brags a few of the most shocking sea shores you'll at any point look at, each with its own one of a kind appeal. Whether you're hoping to get a few waves, absorb the sun, or basically walk around the coastline with your toes in the sand, Sayulita has an ocean side for each mind-set. The principal ocean side, Playa Sayulita, is where all the activity occurs. Here, you'll find an enthusiastic environment with sunbathers relaxing under vivid umbrellas, surfers riding the waves, and merchants offering everything from new coconuts to high quality specialties. It's the ideal spot to watch, get a stunning dusk, or basically loosen up with a decent book. Yet, in the event that you're wanting a smidgen more isolation, dread not - Sayulita has a lot of unlikely treasures ready to be found. Go for a short stroll or bicycle ride along the shoreline, and you'll coincidentally find separated sea shores like Playa Los Muertos or Playa Carricitos, where you can get away from the groups and reconnect with nature. Trust me, there's nothing very like having an unblemished stretch of sand all to yourself, with only the waves hushing you into a condition of unadulterated euphoria.

Presently, we should discuss the food - on the grounds that no excursion to Sayulita would be finished without enjoying the scrumptious culinary pleasures that the town brings to the table. Sayulita is a foodie's heaven, with a different cluster of diners presenting everything from conventional Mexican dishes to global cooking with a neighbourhood bend. One of my number one activities in Sayulita is to set out on a culinary experience through the town's clamouring roads, examining tacos, ceviche, and other nearby fortes en route. Whether you're getting a light meal from a road merchant or feasting at a comfortable ocean front café, you'll be blessed to receive flavours that will tempt your taste buds and leave you hankering more.

Furthermore, we should not disregard the beverages - on the grounds that what's an excursion to Mexico without a couple of margaritas, correct? Sayulita is home to a wealth of oceanside bars and a base where you can taste on reviving mixed drinks while absorbing the sea sees. Whether you favour your margarita on the rocks or frozen, with salt or without, you'll track down no deficiency of choices to extinguish your thirst and cool off from the sweltering climate.

Presently, we should discuss the way of life - on the grounds that Sayulita is far beyond gorgeous sea shores and scrumptious food. It's a town saturated with history and custom, with a dynamic social scene that is simply ready to be investigated. From bright road craftsmanship and vivacious celebrations to conventional music and dance exhibitions, there's continuously something occurring in Sayulita that will catch your consideration and flash your interest. Something I love most about Sayulita is the feeling of the local area that pervades the town.

Wherever you go, you'll be welcomed with comforting grins and well disposed faces, whether you're talking with local people at the market or making new companions at an ocean side huge fire. There's an unmistakable feeling of brotherhood and association here that causes you to feel like you're a piece of something uniquely great.

Furthermore, talking about the local area, Sayulita is additionally known for its obligation to maintainability and ecological protection. The town has done whatever it takes to safeguard its regular excellence and safeguard its fragile environments, with drives like ocean side cleanups, reusing projects, and endeavours to lessen single-use plastics. It's amusing to see a local area meet up to really focus on the climate and guarantee that people in the future can keep on getting a charge out of all that Sayulita brings to the table.

Thus, whether you're looking for experience, unwinding, or just a difference in pace, Sayulita greets you wholeheartedly and welcomes you to encounter the sorcery of this captivating beach front town. From its immaculate sea shores and divine food to its dynamic culture and feeling of the local area, Sayulita has something for everybody. So gather your sacks, abandon your concerns, and come find the reason why Sayulita is genuinely a heaven on the planet.

About Sayulita

Sayulita resembles a secret fortune ready to be found. Situated in the Riviera Nayarit district of Mexico, simply a short drive from Puerto Vallarta, it flaunts all that you could need in a tropical heaven. From unblemished sea shores to rich wildernesses, Sayulita offers an ideal mix of unwinding and experience. Something that struck me the most about Sayulita is its one of a kind mix of societies. It's a blend of local people, expats, and voyagers from everywhere the world, making an energetic and diverse local area. You'll hear Spanish blending with English, French, and, surprisingly, a sprinkle of different dialects, giving the town a global style. The core of Sayulita lies in its bright roads, fixed with store shops, bistros, and eateries. It's the sort of spot where you can go through hours meandering around, absorbing the laid-back air and respecting the nearby work of art. Wherever you look, there's a genuinely new thing to find, whether it's a secret craftsmanship display or a particular road entertainer. Obviously, Sayulita is maybe most popular for its staggering sea shores.

Whether you're a surfer pursuing the ideal wave or a sunbather hoping to unwind, you'll track down your cut of heaven here. The principal ocean side, Playa Sayulita, is ideal for swimming and sunbathing, while neighbouring seashores like Playa Los Muertos offer a calmer departure. Yet, Sayulita isn't just about lazing on the oceanfront (albeit that is most certainly a major piece of it!). The town is likewise a centre for outside exercises, from surfing and paddleboarding to wilderness climbs and zip-lining. One of my #1 encounter was investigating the encompassing wilderness riding a horse, riding through rich vegetation and secret cascades.

With regards to food, Sayulita doesn't dishearten. You'll find everything from conventional Mexican road food to connoisseur eating encounters, with an emphasis on new, neighbourhood fixings.

Make certain to attempt the fish tacos, a Sayulita claim to fame, and wash them down with an invigorating margarita or a cold cerveza. Yet, maybe the best thing about Sayulita is its feeling of the local area. Whether you're a long-lasting occupant or simply going through, you'll feel like a piece of the family from the second you show up. There's continuously something going on, whether it's an ocean side tidy up, a yoga class, or an unrecorded music execution in the town square.

So, Sayulita is a spot like no other. It's a little cut of heaven where time appears to stop, and each second feels like a festival of life. Whether you're searching for experience, unwinding, or just a difference in pace, Sayulita has something for everybody.

Getting to Sayulita

Now that you're tingling to visit Sayulita, let me walk you through how to arrive. While it might feel like an unlikely treasure, getting to Sayulita is quite clear, because of its closeness to Puerto Vallarta. In the event that you're flying in from abroad, your smartest option is to book a trip to Puerto Vallarta Global Air terminal (PVR), which is served by various carriers from around the world. From the air terminal, Sayulita is only a beautiful 45-minute drive away. Whenever you've arrived in Puerto Vallarta, you have a couple of choices for getting to Sayulita:

Rental Car: Leasing a vehicle is maybe the most helpful choice, particularly in the event that you anticipate investigating the encompassing region during your visit. Most significant vehicle rental organisations have workplaces at the air terminal, making it simple to get your vehicle and stir things up around town. The drive from Puerto Vallarta to Sayulita is somewhat direct, with all around kept up with thruways and clear signage en route.

Taxi or Confidential Transfer: On the off chance that you like to pass on the heading to another person, you can sort out for a taxi or confidential exchange from the air terminal to Sayulita. While this choice is more costly than leasing a vehicle, it offers the comfort of house to house administration, and you can simply take it easy as you take in the grand perspectives en route.

Public Transportation: For thrifty voyagers, public transportation is additionally a choice. From the air terminal, you can take a taxi or transport to the close by bus stop, where you can get a neighbourhood transport to Sayulita. While this choice might take a cycle longer than driving or taking a taxi, it's an incredible method for encountering nearby life and talking with individual voyagers en route.

When you show up in Sayulita, you'll know that getting around is kind with your feet.

The town is generally little and walkable, with most attractions, sea shores, and cafés inside simple reach. If you have any desire to investigate further abroad, you can lease a bicycle or a golf truck, or basically jump on one of the neighbourhood transports that run among Sayulita and close by towns.

Chapter 1: Essential Information

Allow me to be your manual for the energetic and mixed heaven that is Sayulita, Mexico. Having invested some energy absorbing the sun, enjoying the flavours, and moving to the rhythms of this otherworldly town, I've assembled all the fundamental data you want to take full advantage of your Sayulita experience. Along these lines, lock in and we should make a plunge!

Area and Overview

Settled on the Pacific shore of Mexico, Sayulita is a bohemian ocean side town that radiates appeal and character every step of the way. Situated in the Riviera Nayarit locale, simply a short drive from Puerto Vallarta, Sayulita is known for its easy going air, shocking sea shores, and lively workmanship scene. Picture this: beautiful roads fixed with store shops, energetic wall paintings decorating each corner, and the sound of crashing waves somewhere far off. Sayulita is where time appears to dial back, permitting you to submerge yourself in the excellence existing apart from everything else completely.

Climate and Climate

Before you gather your sacks for Sayulita, understanding the climate and environment of this tropical paradise is fundamental. Sayulita partakes in a warm and radiant environment all year, with temperatures going from the mid-70s°F to the high 80s°F (mid-20s°C to high 30s°C). The dry season, which runs from November to May, is the most well known opportunity to visit Sayulita. During this time, you can anticipate that a lot of daylight and little should not rain, making it ideal for oceanside days and open air exercises. Notwithstanding, make certain to pack a lot of sunscreen and remain hydrated, as the sun can be serious. The blustery season, which runs from June to October, brings hotter temperatures and intermittent evening showers. While the downpour can be a welcome help from the intensity, it's fundamental to watch out for the weather conditions and be ready for unexpected deluges.

Getting to Sayulita

Presently, we should discuss how to get to this tropical heaven. The nearest significant air terminal to Sayulita is Puerto Vallarta Global Air terminal (PVR), which is found around 40 kilometres south of the town. From the air terminal, you have a few choices for arriving at Sayulita:

Rental Car: Leasing a vehicle is maybe the most helpful choice, particularly in the event that you anticipate investigating the encompassing region during your visit. A few vehicle rental organisations work out of Puerto Vallarta Air terminal, permitting you to get your vehicle upon appearance and make the grand drive to Sayulita. The excursion requires around 45 minutes, contingent upon traffic.

Confidential Transfer: For the individuals who don't really want to drive, confidential exchange administrations are accessible from Puerto Vallarta Air terminal to Sayulita. These administrations offer house to house transportation in cooled vehicles, making for an agreeable and bothersome excursion. While somewhat more costly than different choices, confidential exchanges are an incredible decision for explorers searching for accommodation and solace.

Public Transportation: For economical voyagers, public transportation is likewise a choice. From Puerto Vallarta Air terminal, you can take a taxi or transport to the close by bus stop, where you can get a neighbourhood transport to Sayulita. While this choice might take more time than driving or taking a confidential exchange, it's an extraordinary method for encountering neighbourhood life and setting aside some cash simultaneously.

Accommodation

Whenever you've shown up in Sayulita, you'll require some place to rest your head. Luckily, this town offers an extensive variety of convenience choices to suit each spending plan and inclination. From store lodgings to comfortable guesthouses and sumptuous hotels, there's something for everybody in Sayulita. In the event that you're hoping to drench yourself in the town's bohemian energy, consider remaining in one of the numerous shop lodgings situated in the core of Sayulita.

These sleek properties frequently include brilliant stylistic themes, easygoing environments, and customised administration, making for a critical stay. For those looking for a more isolated retreat, there are a lot of choices right beyond town, settled in the midst of rich wilderness or neglecting the shimmering waters of the Pacific Sea.

Whether you favour a comfortable ocean side home or a sumptuous peak estate, you'll track down a lot of decisions to suit your taste and financial plan in Sayulita.

Neighbourhood Cuisine

No visit to Sayulita would be finished without testing the nearby cooking. Because of its beachfront area and rich culinary practice, Sayulita flaunts an energetic food scene that commends the kinds of Mexico. One of the features of eating in Sayulita is the wealth of new fish, obtained directly from the close by waters. From ceviche and barbecued fish tacos to shrimp mixed drinks and octopus tostadas, there's no lack of delightful fish dishes to attempt. Obviously, no feast in Sayulita would be finished without a reviving margarita or a cold cerveza to wash it down. Whether you favour your beverages on the rocks or mixed with new natural products, you'll track down a lot of choices to extinguish your thirst in Sayulita.

Investigating Sayulita

With its wonderful sea shores, lively craftsmanship scene, and easygoing energy, there's no deficiency of things to see and do in Sayulita. Go through your days absorbing the sun on Playa Sayulita, the town's fundamental ocean side, or investigating the close-by sea shores like Playa Los Muertos and Playa de los Muertos. For the more gutsy voyager, Sayulita offers a lot of chances for open air exercises, from surfing and paddleboarding to zip-covering and wilderness climbs. Investigate the rich wilderness environmental factors on a directed visit, or lease a bicycle and pedal your direction through the grand open country.

Regardless of how you decide to invest your energy in Sayulita, one thing is without a doubt: this beguiling town will catch your heart and pass on you yearning to return over and over.

Travel Tips

In the event that you're arranging an outing to Sayulita, Mexico, let me share some insider tips to assist you with capitalising on your experience. Having invested some energy investigating this dynamic ocean side town, I've gotten a couple of stunts en route that I'm eager to give to you. So get a pen and paper (or your cell phone!) also, how about we plunge into some fundamental travel tips for Sayulita:

Pack Light and Practical: Sayulita is an easygoing ocean side town, so leave the extravagant garments and high heels at home. Select lightweight, breathable textures like cotton and cloth, and remember to pack a lot of sunscreen, a wide-overflowed cap, and shades to shield yourself from the sun.

Remain Hydrated: With its warm and radiant environment, remaining hydrated is key in

Sayulita. Make certain to drink a lot of water over the course of the day, particularly in the event that you're investing energy in the sun or participating in open air exercises. Consider bringing a reusable water jug to top off all through your undertakings.

Cash is King: While numerous organisations in Sayulita acknowledge charge cards, it's generally smart to have some money available, particularly for more modest buys or at neighbourhood markets. ATMs are promptly accessible around, yet it's wise to pull out cash in pesos to keep away from troublesome trade rates.

Get familiar with Some Fundamental Spanish: While English is broadly spoken in Sayulita, realising a few essential Spanish expressions can go far in upgrading your movement experience. Local people feel a debt of gratitude when guests really try to communicate in their language, regardless of whether it's only a couple of straightforward good tidings and merriments.

Regarding the Environment: Sayulita is known for its normal excellence, so make certain to do your part to keep it spotless and flawless. Discard garbage appropriately, keep away from single-use plastics, and think about partaking in oceanside tidy up drives during your visit.

Be Available to New Experiences: Sayulita is a mixture of societies, and no one can really tell what astonishing encounters you could coincidentally find. Whether it's difficult finding another sort of food, figuring out how to surf, or participating in a neighbourhood festivity, be available to venture beyond your usual range of familiarity and embrace the enchantment of Sayulita.

Safety Precautions

While Sayulita is by and large a protected objective for explorers, it's fundamental for avoiding potential risk to guarantee your security and prosperity during your visit. Here are some security tips to remember:

Remain Mindful of Your Surroundings: Like any vacationer location, Sayulita has its portion of unimportant wrongdoing, for example, pickpocketing and robbery. Keep your effects secure and be watchful, particularly in packed regions like business sectors and sea shores.

Utilise Authorised Transportation: While going around Sayulita, it's ideal to utilise authorised taxis or trustworthy transportation administrations. Try not to catch a ride or tolerate rides from outsiders, particularly late around evening time.

Drink Responsibly: Sayulita has a vivacious nightlife scene, with a lot of bars and clubs to appreciate. Notwithstanding, it's fundamental for drink capably and know your cutoff points. Never leave your beverage unattended, and be wary of tolerating drinks from outsiders.

Regarding Nearby Traditions and Laws: Mexico has its own arrangement of regulations and customs, so make certain to dive more deeply into them before your excursion. For instance, public inebriation and medication use are unlawful and can bring about serious results. Be aware of neighbourhood culture and customs consistently.

Remain Protected in the Water: Sayulita's seashores are known for their fantastic surfing and swimming circumstances, however it's fundamental for practice alert, particularly in the event that you're not areas of strength for a. Focus on cautioning banners and flows, and consistently swim close to lifeguard stations if conceivable.

Crisis Contact Information: Before your excursion, make a note of crisis contact data, including the neighbourhood police and clinical benefits. Keep a duplicate of your visa, travel protection subtleties, and significant telephone numbers in a protected spot, for example, your lodging or a solid web-based account.

Cultural Etiquette

Sayulita is an inviting and comprehensive objective, yet regarding neighbourhood customs and behaviour during your visit is fundamental. Here are a few social tips to assist you with exploring your time in Sayulita with effortlessness and regard:

Greetings: In Mexico, good tidings are a fundamental piece of social association. While meeting somebody interestingly, shaking hands and trading pleasantries is standard. Utilise formal titles, for example, "Señor" (Mr.) and "Señora" (Mrs.) except if welcome to utilise first names.

Regard Individual Space: Mexicans will quite often stand nearer together while chatting than individuals from different societies. Regard individual space however don't be astounded in the event that somebody stands nearer to you than you're utilised to.

Eating Etiquette: While feasting in Sayulita, it's standard to trust that the host will welcome you to plunk down prior to sitting down. Keep your hands apparent on the table and try not to lay your elbows on the table while eating.

Tipping: Tipping is standard in Mexico and is valued for good assistance. In cafés, a tip of 10-15% of the complete bill is viewed as standard. Make certain to tip in real money, as Visa tips may not generally go straightforwardly to the staff.

Regard Strict Customs: Mexico is a transcendently Catholic nation, and strict traditions are a fundamental piece of day to day existence. While visiting chapels or strict locales, dress unassumingly and keep away from clear discussions or troublesome way of behaving.

Become familiar with Some Spanish: While many individuals in Sayulita communicate in English, realising a few fundamental Spanish expressions can recognize the neighbourhood culture and make collaborations more pleasant.

Indeed, even basic good tidings and articulations of appreciation can go quite far in cultivating positive associations with local people.

Chapter 2: Accommodation Options

Welcome to Sayulita, where tracking down the ideal spot to rest your head is all essential for the experience! Whether you're longing for a lavish oceanfront manor, a comfortable shop lodging, or a spending plan for a well disposed guesthouse, Sayulita has convenience choices to suit each taste and spending plan. In this way, how about we jump into the universe of Sayulita's facilities and track down the ideal spot for your visit.

Extravagance Manors and Resorts:

In the event that you're hoping to enjoy a definitive extravagance experience, Sayulita's determination of estates and resorts has got you covered. Imagine yourself relaxing by a confidential endlessness pool, tasting mixed drinks with clearing perspectives on the Pacific Sea, and being spoiled with five-star administration. Here are a portion of the top extravagance convenience choices in Sayulita: **Manor Amor:** Roosted on a slope sitting above the town and the sea, Estate Love offers lavish estates and suites with stunning perspectives and upscale conveniences. Loosen up in your confidential dive pool, feast at the on location eatery, and enjoy spa medicines at the health place.

Imanta Resorts Punta de Mita: Found simply a short drive from Sayulita, Imanta Resorts Punta de Mita offers a confined desert garden encompassed by lavish wilderness and immaculate sea shores. Browse sumptuous suites and manors, each with its own confidential patio and open air shower, and appreciate customised administration and top notch conveniences.

Haramara Retreat: For a really exceptional and eco-cognizant extravagance experience, look no farther than Haramara Retreat. Skettled in the midst of 12 sections of land of tropical wilderness, this eco-accommodating retreat offers sumptuous cabanas and suites with staggering sea sees, connoisseur veggie lover cooking, and everyday yoga and reflection classes.

Store Hotels:

Sayulita is home to a beguiling choice of store lodgings, each offering its own special mix of style, solace, and customised administration. From bohemian ocean front hideouts to stylish metropolitan retreats, here are a portion of the top store lodgings in Sayulita:

Inn Hafa: Found simply ventures from the ocean side, Lodging Hafa is a beautiful and diverse store inn with a laid-back vibe. Remain in one of the particularly adorned rooms or suites, loosen up in the housetop pool, and appreciate unrecorded music and occasions at the on location café and bar.

Casa Azul Profundo: This private shop inn offers a peaceful getaway from the hurrying around Sayulita's roads. Set in the midst of lavish tropical nurseries, Casa Azul Profundo highlights a la mode rooms and suites with private porches, a reviving pool, and a serene patio with loungers for relaxing.

Hotelito Los Sueños: Concealed on a tranquil road simply a short stroll from the ocean side, Hotelito Los Sueños offers a comfortable and inviting air with customised administration. Remain in one of the beguiling rooms or suites, loosen up in the rich nursery patio, and appreciate free breakfast served every morning.

Guesthouses and Bed and Breakfasts:

For economical explorers and those looking for a more credible encounter, Sayulita's determination of guesthouses and bed and morning meals offers comfortable facilities with an individual touch. Here are a portion of the top guesthouses and B&Bs in Sayulita:

Casa Maria Elena: This family-run guesthouse offers straightforward and agreeable facilities in the core of Sayulita. Browse comfortable rooms with imparted washrooms or roomy suites to private patios, and appreciate free breakfast served every morning in the yard.

Manors Sayulita: Found simply a short stroll from the ocean side, Estates Sayulita offers reasonable and polished facilities with a casual air. Remain in one of the comfortable visitor rooms or roomy casitas, loosen up in the collective nursery patio, and utilise the common kitchen and bar-b-que region for planning feasts.

Casa Buena Onda: This beguiling bed and breakfast offers a tranquil retreat in the midst of rich tropical gardens simply a short walk around Sayulita's fundamental court. Remain in one of the comfortable rooms or open suites, partake in a free breakfast served every morning on the porch, and loosen up in the reviving pool encompassed by palm trees. *

Get-away Rentals:

For those looking for a usual hangout spot insight, Sayulita offers an extensive variety of excursion rentals, from comfortable ocean front cabins to roomy peak estates. Whether you're travelling alone, with an accomplice, or with a gathering of companions or family, here are a portion of the top excursion rental choices in Sayulita:

Casa Cielo: Roosted on a peak sitting above the town and the sea, Casa Cielo offers stunning perspectives and rich facilities for up to six visitors. Loosen up in the limitlessness pool, feast in the open air on the extensive patio, and partake in the security and isolation of your own confidential retreat.

Casa Nube: This beguiling ocean front cabin offers a comfortable and heartfelt break for couples hoping to loosen up and reconnect. With its natural appeal, staggering sea sees, and direct admittance to the ocean side, Casa Nube is the ideal spot for a heartfelt escape or wedding trip.

Casa Playa: Found simply ventures from the sand, Casa Playa offers roomy facilities for families or gatherings of companions. With its open-idea plan, completely prepared kitchen, and huge outside porch, Casa Playa is the ideal headquarters for a thrilling oceanside get-away in Sayulita.

Hotels & Resorts

On the off chance that you're arranging an excursion to Sayulita, Mexico, and you're in the state of mind for some spoiling and extravagance, then this is your lucky day in light of the fact that Sayulita brags a phenomenal choice lodgings and resorts that will cause you to feel like eminence. Allow me to walk you through a portion of the top choices:

Estate Amor: Settled on a slope sitting above the town and the sea, Manor Love is a cut of heaven. With its dazzling perspectives, rich facilities, and immaculate help, it's no big surprise why this retreat is a #1 among voyagers. Browse various estates and suites, each wonderfully delegated and outfitted with present day conveniences. Loosen up by the vastness pool, enjoy a back rub at the spa, or relish scrumptious food at the on location café. Estate Love really offers a stand-out encounter that you will probably remember forever.

Imanta Resorts Punta de Mita: Assuming you're searching for a definitive extravagance escape, look no farther than Imanta Resorts Punta de Mita. Found simply a short drive from Sayulita, this isolated retreat offers unparalleled security and peacefulness. Remain in one of the lavish suites or manors, each fastidiously planned with regular materials and shocking sea sees. Go through your days relaxing by the limitlessness pool, investigating the unblemished sea shores, or enjoying connoisseur cooking at the on location café. Imanta Resorts Punta de Mita is the ideal objective for knowing voyagers looking for a genuinely extraordinary encounter.

Haramara Retreat: For a remarkable and eco-cognizant extravagance experience, consider remaining at Haramara Retreat. Settled in the midst of 12 sections of land of rich tropical wilderness, this eco-accommodating hotel offers a quiet and peaceful getaway from the rushing about of day to day existence. Look over different delightful cabanas and suites, each hand-assembled utilising conventional development procedures and including shocking sea sees. Practice yoga and reflection in the outdoors studio, feast on flavorful vegan food made with new, privately obtained fixings, and revive your body and soul with comprehensive spa medicines. Haramara Retreat is a safe-haven for those looking for harmony, congruity, and association with nature.

Vacation Rentals

In the event that you're searching for a usual hangout spot during your visit in Sayulita, excursion rentals are a fabulous choice.

Whether you're travelling alone, with an accomplice, or with a gathering of companions or family, Sayulita offers an extensive variety of excursion rental choices to suit each taste and spending plan. Here are a portion of the top decisions:

Casa Cielo: Roosted on a peak sitting above the town and the sea, Casa Cielo offers stunning perspectives and rich facilities for up to six visitors. This dazzling get-away rental elements a roomy open-idea living region, a completely prepared kitchen, and a confidential endlessness pool encompassed by lavish tropical nurseries. Loosen up on the extensive patio, eat outdoors under the stars, and absorb the excellence of Sayulita from your own confidential retreat.

Casa Nube: In the event that you're looking for a comfortable and heartfelt break, Casa Nube is the ideal decision. This beguiling ocean front home offers staggering sea sees and direct admittance to the sand. With its natural appeal, agreeable decorations, and tranquil feel, Casa Nube is the best spot for a heartfelt escape or wedding trip. Go through your days relaxing on the confidential porch, swimming in the completely clear waters of the Pacific, and watching the nightfall over the sea.

Casa Playa: Found simply ventures from the ocean side, Casa Playa is an optimal getaway rental for families or gatherings of companions. This open and slick estate includes different rooms, a completely prepared kitchen, and an enormous outside porch with a bar-b-que barbecue and eating region. Go through your days surfing, swimming, and investigating all that Sayulita brings to the table, then return to Casa Playa to unwind and loosen up in solace and style.

Hostels & Guesthouses

On the off chance that you're going on a careful spending plan or hoping to associate with individual explorers, lodgings and guesthouses are a fabulous choice in Sayulita. These spending plan cordial facilities offer agreeable beds, shared spaces, and a well disposed environment that is ideal for solo explorers or those hoping to make new companions. Here are a few top decisions:

Casa Maria Elena: This family-run guesthouse offers straightforward and reasonable facilities in the core of Sayulita. Browse comfortable rooms with imparted restrooms or open suites to private patios. Appreciate free breakfast served every morning in the yard, loosen up in the mutual parlour region, and trade travel stories with individual visitors.

Manors Sayulita: Found simply a short stroll from the ocean side, Estates Sayulita offers spending plan cordial facilities with a laid-back vibe. Remain in one of the comfortable visitor rooms or roomy casitas, loosen up in the collective nursery yard, and utilise the common kitchen and bar-b-que region for getting ready feasts. With its accommodating staff and inviting air, Estates Sayulita is an extraordinary choice for economical voyagers.

Casa Buena Onda: Concealed on a peaceful road simply a short walk around Sayulita's primary square, Casa Buena Onda offers agreeable and reasonable facilities with an individual touch. Remain in one of the comfortable rooms or roomy suites, partake in a free breakfast served every morning on the patio, and loosen up in the reviving pool encompassed by rich tropical nurseries. With its casual climate and well disposed staff, Casa Buena Onda is an extraordinary decision for explorers looking for a usual hangout spot in Sayulita.

Chapter 3: Top Tourist Attractions

Welcome to Sayulita, where each corner is a fortune ready to be found! From flawless sea shores and lavish wilderness to dynamic business sectors and social milestones, Sayulita offers an abundance of attractions that will charm and motivate explorers, everything being equal. Thus, how about we plunge into a portion of the top vacation spots that you won't have any desire to miss during your visit:

Playa Sayulita: We should begin with the crown gem of Sayulita - its lovely sea shores. Playa Sayulita is the principal oceanside around and is a centre of movement, with brilliant sands, perfectly clear waters, and a lot of room for sunbathing, swimming, and surfing. Whether you're a carefully prepared surfer getting waves or a scavenger absorbing the sun, Playa Sayulita is the ideal spot to go through a lethargic day by the ocean.

Playa de los Muertos: Simply a short stroll from the fundamental ocean side untruths Playa de los Muertos, or "Ocean side of the Dead." Regardless of its unpropitious name, this separated inlet is an unlikely treasure with turquoise waters, emotional stone developments, and a quiet air. Pack an outing, bring your swimming stuff, and go through the day investigating this lovely oceanside heaven.

Sayulita Plaza: No visit to Sayulita would be finished without a walk around the town's enchanting fundamental court. Encircled by bright structures, energetic bistros, and clamouring markets, Sayulita Square is the essence of the town. Sit down on a seat, taste on a reviving agua fresca, and absorb the lively environment as local people and sightseers approach their day.

Mercado del Pueblo: For a sample of neighbourhood culture and cooking, make certain to visit Mercado del Pueblo, Sayulita's week after week ranchers' market. Held each Friday morning in the town square, this clamouring market includes a wide assortment of new produce, distinctive products, high quality specialties, and scrumptious road food. Test neighbourhood strengths like tamales, tacos, and new natural product smoothies, and get extraordinary trinkets to bring back home with you.

Sayulita Road Art: Sayulita is known for its lively road craftsmanship scene, with brilliant wall paintings decorating structures all through the town. Take an independent strolling visit and find works by neighbourhood and global specialists, portraying everything from eccentric animals to intriguing political proclamations. Remember to bring your camera - you'll need to catch these Instagram-commendable minutes!

Just a little of experience and investigation, go to Punta Sayulita, a rough headland situated at the southern end of the fundamental ocean side. Follow the picturesque wilderness trail that breezes its direction along the shore, going through rich tropical vegetation and offering amazing perspectives on the sea beneath. Look out for untamed life like iguanas, tropical birds, and even whales throughout the cold weather months.

Sayulita Nayarit Social Center: Drench yourself in Sayulita's rich social legacy at the Sayulita Nayarit Social Center. Situated in the core of town, this dynamic social centre has various occasions, studios, and shows that praise the practices, expressions, and artworks of the locale. From conventional dance exhibitions to ceramics classes and cooking shows, there's continuously something invigorating occurring at the Social Community.

Surfing and Water Sports: Sayulita is renowned for its fantastic riding conditions, making it a central hub for water sports lovers from around the world. Whether you're an old pro or a novice hoping to get your most memorable wave, Sayulita offers surf examples, board rentals, and a lot of chances to ride the waves. As well as surfing, you can likewise take a stab at paddleboarding, kayaking, swimming, and fishing – the potential outcomes are inestimable!

Marietas Islands: For a road trip you will always remember, bounce on a boat and investigate the stunning magnificence of the Marietas Islands. Found simply off the shoreline of Sayulita, this safeguarded marine save is home to a wealth of untamed life, including dolphins, ocean turtles, and fascinating birds. Swim through secret caverns, swim in perfectly clear waters, and wonder about the shocking normal excellence of this distant island heaven.

Yelapa: In the event that you're hoping to get away from the rushing about of Sayulita for a day, consider going on a boat outing to the beguiling town of Yelapa. Found south of Sayulita along the tough shore, Yelapa is an unexpected, yet invaluable treasure with perfect sea shores, rich wilderness, and a laid-back vibe. Go through the day relaxing on the oceanfront, investigating the town, and absorbing the excellence of this segregated heaven.

Sayulita Beach

Sayulita Ocean side - the heartbeat of this beguiling Mexican town. Allow me to take you on an excursion to this cut of heaven where sun, sand, and surf combine to make a really supernatural encounter.

Envision yourself venturing onto the delicate, brilliant sands of Sayulita Ocean side, experiencing the glow of the sun on your skin and the delicate breeze in your hair. The sound of crashing waves consumes the atmosphere as you take in the all encompassing perspective on the turquoise waters loosening up before you. Whether you're a sun admirer, a water sports lover, or essentially somebody who loves to absorb the magnificence of nature, Sayulita Ocean side has something for everybody.

Something that makes Sayulita Ocean side so extraordinary is its easygoing energy. Not at all like a portion of the more packed traveller objections, Sayulita Ocean side has figured out how to keep up with its vagueness and appeal. Here, you'll find local people and guests blending together, sharing stories, giggling, and a profound appreciation for the regular excellence that encompasses them.

As you investigate the Sayulita Ocean side, you'll experience a lively embroidery of sights, sounds, and encounters. Families assemble sandcastles along the coastline, youngsters sprinkle in the shallows, and couples walk connected at the hip along the water's edge. Surfers paddle out past the breakers, anxious to get the ideal wave, while oceanside merchants meander the sands offering all that from new natural products to hand tailored creations.

Yet, in addition to the exercises make Sayulita Ocean side so exceptional - likewise the normal excellence encompasses you. Transcending palm trees influence the breeze, giving shade and asylum from the sun. Pelicans coast effortlessly above, plunging into the water to get their next feast. What's more, assuming you're fortunate, you could try and recognize dolphins playing somewhere far off or ocean turtles settling on the sand.

As the day attracts nearby, Sayulita Ocean side takes on a supernatural quality. The sunset projects a brilliant gleam over the sea, painting the sky with shades of orange, pink, and purple. Local people and guests alike accumulate on the sand to watch the display, sharing stories and giggling as they bid goodbye to one more lovely day in heaven.

Be that as it may, the magnificence of Sayulita Ocean side reaches out a long way past its sandy shores - it's likewise a centre of movement and fervour. From surfing and paddleboarding to oceanside volleyball and yoga, there's no deficiency of ways of remaining engaged. Furthermore, on the off chance that you're feeling daring, you might lease a kayak or stand-up paddleboard to investigate the shoreline or take a stab at swimming to find the beautiful marine life that lies underneath the surface.

As the stars sparkle above and the huge fires spring up along the coastline, Sayulita Ocean side takes on another energy. Companions accumulate around the glinting blazes, sharing stories, giggling, and maybe a couple of cold cervezas as they watch the waves come in. What's more, as you sink into the sand, looking up at the night sky and paying attention to the sea, you can't resist the urge to feel a profound feeling of harmony and satisfaction wash over you.

So on the off chance that you're at any point needing a little cut of heaven, look no farther than Sayulita Ocean side. With its dazzling normal magnificence, lively energy, and vast open doors for experience, an objective will catch your heart and pass on you yearning to return over and over.

Plaza Sayulita

Welcome to Square Sayulita – the thumping heart of this lively Mexican town. From brilliant business sectors to exuberant bistros, this clamouring square is the ideal spot to submerge yourself in the neighbourhood culture and absorb the lively energy of Sayulita.

As you step into Court Sayulita, you'll wind up encompassed by a kaleidoscope of sights, sounds, and scents. Beautiful structures line the cobblestone roads, their exteriors enhanced with complex wall paintings and dynamic road workmanship. The air is loaded up with the alluring smells of newly blended espresso, sizzling tacos, and fragrant blossoms, enticing you to investigate further.

At the focal point of the court, you'll find a clamouring market where nearby craftsmans and merchants grandstand their products. From hand tailored adornments and woven materials to stoneware, canvases, and other extraordinary fortunes, there's a here thing to suit each taste and spending plan. Take as much time as necessary meandering through the slows down, visiting with the well disposed sellers, and finding stand-out gifts to bring back home with you.

Encompassing the market, you'll track down various bistros, cafés, and bars where you can refuel and re-energize. Take a seat at one of the outside decks and partake in a comfortable dinner while absorbing the energetic climate of the square. Whether you're longing for conventional Mexican food, new fish, or global charge, you'll track down a lot of choices to entice your taste buds.

Be that as it may, Court Sayulita is something other than a spot to shop and eat - it's likewise a centre of action and diversion.

Over the course of the day, you'll track down unrecorded music, road entertainers, and comprehensive developments occurring in the square, adding to its lively energy and merry climate. From customary dance exhibitions to unrecorded music shows, there's continuously something energising occurring in Square Sayulita.

As the sun sets and the gleaming lights of the square show some major signs of life, Court Sayulita takes on an otherworldly quality. Local people and guests assemble in the square, tasting mixed drinks, sharing stories, and moving under the stars. The sound of chuckling consumes the space as the night wakes up with energy, making recollections that will endure forever.

So in the event that you're hoping to drench yourself in the lively culture and energy of Sayulita, make certain to visit Court Sayulita. With its bright business sectors, exuberant bistros, and happy environment, it's the ideal spot to encounter the genuine substance of this enchanting Mexican town.

Sayulita Farmers Market

Welcome to the Sayulita Ranchers Market – a lively and clamouring centre point of action where local people and guests meet up to commend the overflow of new produce, distinctive products, and culinary pleasures that make Sayulita such an extraordinary spot.

As you meander through the market, you'll wind up encompassed by a kaleidoscope of varieties, fragrances, and flavours. New products of the soil pour out from containers and cartons, their lively shades enticing you to investigate. From delicious mangoes and ready avocados to stout tomatoes and fresh greens, the abundance of the land is on full display.

However, the Sayulita Ranchers Market is something other than a put to load up on food – it's likewise a mother lode of high quality merchandise and hand tailored treasures. Nearby craftsmans exhibit their abilities, selling everything from carefully assembled gems and woven materials to ceramics, canvases, and other one of a kind manifestations. Whether you're looking for a unique trinket or an exceptional gift, you're certain to track down something that gets your attention.

As you investigate the market, make certain to test a portion of the delightful road food and tidbits on offer. From flavorful tacos and tamales to sweet baked goods and new crushed juices, there's a thing here to fulfil each hankering. Have a seat at one of the open air tables and partake in a relaxed feast while absorbing the exuberant air of the market.

Sayulita Street Art

Sayulita's roads resemble an outside display, with dynamic paintings and perplexing spray painting embellishing walls and structures all through the town. From unusual animals to provocative political proclamations, the road workmanship in Sayulita mirrors the imagination and soul of its occupants.

As you meander through the cobblestone roads and limited rear entryways of Sayulita, you'll experience a kaleidoscope of varieties and plans every step of the way. Intense brushstrokes and many-sided stencils cover walls, entryways, and, surprisingly, utility boxes, changing conventional spaces into masterpieces.

One of my #1 thing about Sayulita's road workmanship is its variety. Every painting recounts a special story, mirroring the viewpoints and encounters of the craftsmen who made them. A few pieces are perky and cheerful, highlighting eccentric characters and hallucinogenic examples, while others are more pensive and reflective, resolving social and natural issues confronting the local area.

Be that as it may, regardless of the style or topic, Sayulita's road craftsmanship never neglects to charm and motivate. It's a visual banquet for the faculties, offering vast open doors for investigation and revelation. Also, in light of the fact that the craftsmanship is continually developing, there's continuously a genuinely new thing to see and experience each time you visit.

One of the most incredible ways of investigating Sayulita's road craftsmanship scene is walking. Take an independent strolling visit and meander through the town at your own speed, permitting yourself to become mixed up in its dynamic roads and back streets. Hide your eyes stripped for unlikely treasures in surprising corners, and don't hesitate for even a moment to start up a discussion with nearby craftsmen or occupants - no one can really tell what entrancing stories you could uncover.

Whether you're a craftsmanship devotee or essentially somebody who values magnificence in the entirety of its structures, Sayulita's road workmanship scene makes certain to have an enduring effect. So get your camera, trim up your strolling shoes, and prepare to leave on a visual experience not at all like some other.

Monkey Mountain Hike

For those looking for experience and stunning perspectives, the Monkey Mountain climb is a must-do action in Sayulita. Found simply relatively close to the town community, Monkey Mountain - otherwise called Cerro del Mono - offers climbers the opportunity to drench themselves in nature and witness all encompassing vistas of the encompassing scene.

The climb starts at the edge of Sayulita, where a very much checked trail leads you through rich tropical wilderness and tough territory. As you rise the mountain, you'll be blessed to receive shocking perspectives on the town underneath, with its bright housetops and flawless sea shores loosening up to the skyline.

En route, watch out for local verdure - from transcending palm trees and dynamic blossoms to intriguing birds and butterflies. You might try and catch a brief look at the slippery white-confronted capuchin monkeys that call Monkey Mountain home, swinging through the trees above.

As you close to the highest point, the path becomes more extreme and seriously testing, however the work is definitely justified. At the top, you'll be compensated with all encompassing perspectives on Sayulita, the encompassing wilderness, and the shimmering waters of the Pacific Sea. A sight will blow your mind and leave you feeling elated and invigorated.

Set aside some margin to absorb the excellence of your environmental factors, snap some photographs to catch the occasion, and maybe partake in a merited excursion lunch prior to starting your drop. What's more, as you advance down the mountain, pause for a minute to consider the experience and value the regular magnificence that encompasses you.

The Monkey Mountain climb is a difficult yet remunerating experience that offers explorers the opportunity to associate with nature, stretch their boundaries, and witness probably the most dynamite seen in Sayulita. So trim up your climbing boots, pack a lot of water and tidbits, and prepare for a remarkable excursion into the core of the Mexican wilderness.

Hidden Beaches

Sayulita is renowned for its staggering sea shores, however the absolute most gorgeous and disconnected spots are many times off in an unexpected direction. From stowed bays to secret stretches of sand, Sayulita's secret seashores offer the ideal getaway for those hoping to unwind, loosen up, and submerge themselves in the regular magnificence of the shoreline.

One of my #1 secret sea shore in Sayulita is Playa de los Muertos, or "Ocean side of the Dead." Notwithstanding its unfavourable name, this disconnected bay is a genuine unlikely treasure, with turquoise waters, sensational stone developments, and a peaceful environment that feels like a world away from the hurrying around town.

To arrive at Playa de los Muertos, you'll have to follow a short path that breezes its direction through rich wilderness and rough landscape. As you arise onto the ocean side, you'll be welcomed by a stunning display of unblemished sands and completely clear waters – the ideal spot for sunbathing, swimming, and swimming.

One more unlikely treasure worth investigating is Playa Carricitos, a segregated oceanside found simply a short drive or climb from Sayulita. With its brilliant sands, delicate waves, and lavish tropical environmental elements, Playa Carricitos feels like a genuine heaven. Pack a cookout, bring your swimming stuff, and go through the day absorbing the sun and surf at this secret desert spring.

For those ready to wander a piece farther abroad, Playa Patzcuaro is one more secret oceanside worth searching out. Situated around 30 minutes south of Sayulita, this perfect stretch of sand offers staggering perspectives, quiet waters, and a lot of room to fan out and unwind. Load a cooler with bites and beverages, lease an ocean side umbrella and seats from a neighbourhood merchant, and go through the day partaking in the harmony and peacefulness of this unlikely treasure.

Chapter 4: Activities and Adventures

Welcome to the dynamic universe of Sayulita, where experience coaxes from each corner! As somebody who has submerged myself in the heap exercises and encounters this enchanting Mexican town brings to the table, let me be your manual for the exhilarating undertakings that look for you.

Surfing: Ah, surfing – the heartbeat of Sayulita. Whether you're an old pro or an inquisitive fledgling, Sayulita's waves are calling out to you. Snatch a board, slap on some sunscreen, and make a beeline for Playa Sayulita, where the Pacific Sea offers the ideal jungle gym for wave riders, all things considered. On the off chance that you're new to the game, dread not - there are a lot of surf schools and educators prepared to get you up on your feet and riding the waves like an ace. Furthermore, for those looking for a test, close-by breaks like La Lancha and Punta de Mita offer bigger grows and more adrenaline-sipping rides.

Stand-Up Paddleboarding (SUP): In the event that riding isn't your thing, why not take a stab at stand-up paddleboarding (SUP)? Skim along the quiet waters of Sayulita Sound, taking in the beautiful shore and spotting marine life underneath. It's a tranquil and reflective method for interfacing with nature and absorbing the magnificence of Sayulita's shore. You can lease a paddleboard from one of the numerous neighbourhood administrators or join a directed visit for a more vivid encounter.

Snorkelling and Scuba Diving: Plunge underneath the surface and find the lively submerged world that lies simply seaward. Sayulita is encircled by perfectly clear waters overflowing with marine life, making it a heaven for swimmers and scuba jumpers. Join a boat visit to investigate nearby reefs and submerged caves, where you can swim close by beautiful coral, exotic fish, and even ocean turtles on the off chance that you're fortunate. With its warm waters and different biological systems, Sayulita offers remarkable swimming and jumping encounters for swashbucklers, everything being equal.

Hiking and Nature Walks: Ribbon up your climbing boots and adventure into the rich wildernesses and rough mountains that encompass Sayulita. From delicate nature strolls to testing journeys, there are trails to suit each degree of wellness and experience. One well known climb is to the culmination of Monkey Mountain, where you'll be compensated with all encompassing perspectives on the town and shoreline underneath. Or on the other hand, investigate the secret cascades and mystery swimming openings concealed in the wilderness, where you can chill with a reviving dunk in the perfectly clear waters.

Zip Lining: Get your adrenaline syphoning with an undeniably exhilarating zip lining experience through the wilderness shelter. Fly through the treetops on thrilling zip lines, rising above lavish valleys and gorges as you take in stunning perspectives on the encompassing scene. Numerous neighbourhood eco-experience parks offer zip fixing visits alongside other invigorating exercises like rappelling, rock climbing, and shade strolls. It's an elating method for encountering the excellence of Sayulita's regular environmental factors from an entirely different viewpoint.

Horseback Riding: Seat up and investigate the picturesque wide open encompassing Sayulita riding a horse. Directed horseback riding visits take you along quiet paths and disconnected sea shores, where you can absorb the excellence of the scene and spot local untamed life en route. Whether you're running through the wilderness or dashing along the coastline, horseback riding offers an extraordinary and critical method for encountering the excellence of Sayulita's open country.

Yoga and Wellbeing Retreats: Find your harmony in Sayulita with a yoga or health retreat that joins unwinding, restoration, and investigation. Numerous neighbourhood resorts and retreat focuses offer yoga classes, reflection meetings, spa medicines, and comprehensive health programs intended to feed the body, psyche, and soul. Whether you're a carefully prepared yogi or new to the training, Sayulita gives the ideal scenery for tracking down balance and internal harmony.

Fishing Charters: Set forth on the Pacific Sea for a day of remote ocean fishing experiences. Join a fishing sanction and take a shot at getting major game fish like marlin, sailfish, fish, and mahi. Experienced skippers and group individuals will direct you to the best fishing spots and give all the essential gear, guaranteeing an intriguing and vital fishing experience for fishermen, everything being equal.

Cooking Classes and Food Tours: Submerge yourself in the kinds of Mexican food with a preparing class or food visit in Sayulita. Figure out how to get ready customary dishes like ceviche, tacos, and mole from nearby gourmet specialists and culinary specialists, utilising new, privately obtained fixings. Investigate the town's business sectors, road food slows down, and cafés to test different real Mexican flavours and find the culinary joys of Sayulita.

Cultural Studios and Experiences: Jump profound into the rich social legacy of Sayulita with vivid studios and encounters that exhibit the customs, expressions, and artworks of the locale. Figure out how to make customary crafted works like earthenware, winding around, and adornments from neighbourhood craftsmans, or partake in social exercises like dance classes, music exhibitions, and tequila tastings. These involved encounters furnish an exceptional chance to interface with the nearby local area and gain knowledge into the dynamic culture of Sayulita.

Surfing

The quintessential Sayulita experience. Envision yourself remaining on a board, feeling the surge of the sea underneath you as you float easily across the water's surface. Sayulita's waves are unbelievable among surfers, offering the ideal blend of consistency, size, and shape for riders, everything being equal.

Fledglings, dread not - Sayulita is a phenomenal spot to figure out how to surf. There are various surf schools and teachers covering the ocean side, prepared to furnish you with the abilities and certainty you really want to get your most memorable wave. With patient direction and master guidance, you'll spring up and ride the waves quickly.

For accomplished surfers, Sayulita offers various breaks to suit various inclinations and expertise levels. Playa Sayulita, the town's primary oceanside, includes a smooth, sandy-lined break that is ideal for novices and longboarders. Close by breaks like La Lancha and Punta de Mita offer bigger grows and additional difficult waves for transitional and high level surfers looking for an adrenaline rush.

However, surfing in Sayulita is about something beyond getting waves - it's tied in with drenching yourself in the laid-back surf culture that pervades the town. After a morning meeting in the water, go to one of the ocean front bistros or taco stands to refuel with a delightful feast and trade stories with individual surfers. The feeling of brotherhood and shared stir up is unmistakable, making each surf meeting in Sayulita a noteworthy encounter.

Stand-up Paddleboarding

In the event that you're searching for a more loosened up method for partaking in the water, stand-up paddleboarding (SUP) is the ideal choice. Float along the peaceful waters of Sayulita Straight, taking in the grand shore and absorbing the warm Mexican sun.

Perhaps the best thing about SUP in Sayulita is the flexibility of the action. Whether you're a novice searching for a relaxed oar or an accomplished paddler looking for a test, there's something for everybody. You can investigate the quiet waters of the narrows, paddle out to local sea shores and bays, or even attempt SUP yoga for an interesting and peaceful experience on the water.

Numerous nearby administrators offer SUP rentals and directed visits, making it simple to get out on the water and investigate at your own speed. Whether you're rowing solo or joining a gathering journey, SUP in Sayulita is a tranquil and compensating method for interfacing with nature and partake in the magnificence of the shore.

Snorkeling and Diving

For the people who like to investigate the submerged world, Sayulita offers the absolute best swimming and jumping open doors in Mexico. With its perfectly clear waters, dynamic coral reefs, and plentiful marine life, Sayulita is a heaven for submerged lovers, all things considered.

Get your cover, snorkel, and balance, and get ready to be flabbergasted by the vivid coral nurseries and exotic fish that occupy Sayulita's submerged jungle gym. Join a swimming visit to investigate close by reefs and rough outcrops, where you can swim close by schools of vivid fish, spot beams floating effortlessly across the sandy base, and perhaps experience an ocean turtle or two.

For those looking for a more profound plunge, Sayulita likewise offers phenomenal scuba jumping open doors. Join a jump contract and investigate submerged caverns, wrecks, and coral nurseries overflowing with life. Whether you're a fledgling jumper or an accomplished submerged pioneer, Sayulita's different plunge locales offer something for everybody.

One of the features of making a plunge in Sayulita is the opportunity to experience bigger marine species like manta rays, whale sharks, and even humpback whales throughout the cold weather months. These glorious animals relocate through the waters of Sayulita Narrows, giving remarkable experiences to fortunate jumpers and swimmers.

Yoga and Wellness

Sayulita - a shelter for those looking for equilibrium, serenity, and restoration for the whole self. As somebody who has enjoyed the yoga and wellbeing contributions of this beguiling Mexican town, let me guide you through the tranquil encounters that anticipate.

Sayulita's easy going environment and regular magnificence make it the ideal setting for yoga and wellbeing withdrawals. Envision yourself rehearsing sun welcome on an unblemished ocean side at the crack of dawn, with the sound of crashing waves and the glow of the sun wrapping you one might say of harmony and peacefulness. Whether you're a carefully prepared yogi or new to the training, Sayulita offers an assortment of yoga classes and withdraws to suit each level and inclination.

Numerous neighbourhood resorts and retreat focuses offer everyday yoga classes in different styles, from vinyasa stream to hatha yoga, yin yoga, and that's just the beginning. These classes are driven by experienced teachers who give direction and backing to professionals, everything being equal, guaranteeing a safe and enhancing experience for everybody. Envision beginning your day with a delicate yoga work on ignoring the sea, feeling grounded and focused as you get ready to investigate all that Sayulita brings to the table.

Notwithstanding day to day yoga classes, Sayulita is likewise home to various health specialists and comprehensive healers who offer different administrations to advance wellbeing and prosperity. Indulge yourself with a loosening up rub, needle therapy meeting, or energy mending treatment to loosen up and let strain out of both body and psyche. A large number utilise normal and privately obtained fixings in their medicines, adding an additional layer of realness to the experience.

For those hoping to jump further into their wellbeing process, Sayulita additionally offers multi-day yoga and wellbeing withdrawals that consolidate yoga, reflection, solid cooking, and other comprehensive practices to support the body, brain, and soul. These retreats happen in gorgeous and tranquil settings, permitting members to detach from the anxieties of day to day existence and reconnect with themselves and nature.

Whether you're looking for unwinding, revival, or just a break from the hurrying around of day to day existence, Sayulita's yoga and wellbeing contributions give the ideal chance to feed your body, brain, and soul in a serene and strong climate.

Horseback Riding

There's something really mysterious about investigating the beautiful wide open encompassing Sayulita riding a horse. As somebody who has outfitted up and wandered into the rich wildernesses and flawless seashores of this lovely Mexican town, let me share with you the elating experience of horseback riding in Sayulita.

Sayulita offers an assortment of directed horseback riding visits that take care of riders of all levels, from fledglings to experienced equestrians. Whether you're jogging along quiet paths or dashing along the coastline, horseback riding permits you to submerge yourself in the regular excellence of Sayulita's scene while fashioning a profound association with these magnificent creatures.

One famous horseback riding objective in Sayulita is the encompassing wilderness, where direct visits take you along winding paths that wander through lavish foliage and transcending trees. Look out for local untamed life like birds, butterflies, and, surprisingly, a periodic iguana or coatimundi as you investigate the wilderness riding a horse.

For those looking for a more seaside experience, horseback riding visits along the ocean side offer stunning perspectives on the Pacific Sea and the potential chance to feel the breeze in your hair as you run along the sandy shores. Envision the excitement of riding close by the crashing waves, feeling the cadenced beat of your pony's hooves against the sand as you take in the sights and hints of the shoreline.

Many horseback riding visits additionally incorporate stops at grand perspectives, stowed cascades, and detached sea shores, permitting you to find unexpected, yet invaluable treasures and mystery recognises that must be gotten to riding a horse. It's a genuinely vivid method for encountering the excellence and variety of Sayulita's scene, all while making recollections that will endure forever.

Whether you're a carefully prepared rider or a fledgling equestrian, horseback riding in Sayulita offers a special and extraordinary method for interfacing with nature, investigating the open country, and experiencing the wizardry of this enchanting Mexican town.

Fishing Charters

Set forth on the shimmering waters of the Pacific Sea for a day of remote ocean fishing experiences in Sayulita. As somebody who has projected my line into the sea and pulled in the enormous catch, let me share with you the energy and rush of fishing contracts in Sayulita.

Sayulita is encircled by probably the best fishing grounds in Mexico, making it a heaven for fishermen, all things considered. Joining a fishing sanction is the ideal method for encountering the excitement of remote ocean fishing while at the same time investigating the dazzling shoreline and partaking in the warm heat and humidity.

Numerous nearby administrators offer half-day and entire day fishing sanctions that take special care of both amateur and experienced fishermen. Whether you're focusing on major game fish like marlin, sailfish, and fish, or projecting for more modest species like dorado, snapper, and roosterfish, Sayulita's waters are overflowing with marine life ready to be gotten.

Experienced chiefs and group individuals will direct you to the best fishing spots and give all the essential hardware, including poles, reels, snare, and tackle. They'll likewise share their insight and ability to assist you with pulling in the large one, offering tips and strategies to expand your odds of coming out on top.

As you journey along the shore, look out for dolphins, ocean turtles, and even whales throughout the cold weather months. These great animals frequently show up in Sayulita's waters, adding an additional layer of energy and miracle to your fishing experience.

Chapter 5: Dining and Nightlife

Welcome to the tasty universe of Sayulita, where each feast is a culinary experience and consistently is loaded up with fervour and energy. As somebody who has enjoyed the different flavours and moved the night away in this energetic Mexican town, let me be your manual for the feasting and nightlife scene that is standing by.

Dining:

Sayulita is a food sweetheart's heaven, offering a delectable exhibit of culinary pleasures to fulfil each sense of taste and hankering. From customary Mexican cooking to global flavours and in the middle between, Sayulita's feasting scene is however different as it very well might be delectable.

We should begin with breakfast - the main feast of the day. Whether you're needing a good Mexican breakfast of huevos rancheros and chilaquiles or something lighter like new leafy foods, Sayulita takes care of you. Go to one of the neighbourhood bistros or ocean front cafés for a relaxed morning feast, joined by some newly fermented espresso or an invigorating agua fresca.

For lunch, why not enjoy some real road tacos or fish ceviche? Sayulita's roads are fixed with taco stands and fish slows down serving up delectable dishes made with new, privately obtained fixings. Pull up a stool, request a plate of tacos al minister or shrimp tostadas, and relish the kinds of Mexico in each nibble.

As the sun sets, now is the right time to begin pondering supper. Sayulita flaunts a different feasting scene with choices going from upscale cafés to relaxed restaurants and in the middle between. Whether you're in the state of mind for connoisseur cooking, wood-terminated pizza, or ranch-to-table admission, you'll track down everything in Sayulita.

One of my number one eating encounters in Sayulita is feasting on new fish by the ocean side. Numerous oceanfront cafés offer tables right on the sand, permitting you to feast with your toes in the sand and the waves crashing behind the scenes. It's the ideal method for finishing a day of sun, surf, and investigation.

What's more, we should not disregard dessert – in light of the fact that no feast is finished without something sweet. Sayulita is home to a few bread kitchens and pastry shops presenting heavenly deals like churros, frozen yoghurt, and cakes. Indulge yourself with a sweet guilty pleasure and fulfil your sweet tooth prior to going out to investigate Sayulita's energetic nightlife scene.

Nightlife:

At the point when the sun goes down, Sayulita wakes up with energy and fervour, offering an energetic nightlife scene that is not to be missed. Whether you're searching for a calm mixed drink, an ocean front bar, or a clamouring club, Sayulita has something for everybody.

Begin your night with a dusk mixed drink at one of the town's oceanfront bars or housetop lounges. Taste on a margarita or mojito as you watch the sun sink underneath the skyline, projecting a brilliant shine over the sea and the town beneath. It's the ideal method for loosening up and absorbing the magnificence of the night prior to the night's celebrations start.

As the night advances, Sayulita's roads wake up with music, giggling, and moving. Make a beeline for the town square, known as Court Sayulita, where local people and vacationers assemble to mingle and appreciate unrecorded music and diversion. Sit down on one of the seats or dance under the stars as nearby artists and entertainers make that big appearance.

Assuming you're in the state of mind for moving, Sayulita has a few clubs and bars where you can move the night away to the hints of live DJs and groups. From reggae and salsa to electronic and rock, there's no deficiency of music and dance floors to keep you moving until the early hours of the morning.

For a more easygoing night, why not go to one of Sayulita's comfortable wine bars or distinctive mezcalerias? Taste on a glass of wine or test a portion of Mexico's best mezcal as you blend with local people and individual voyagers, sharing stories and making new companions en route.

What's more, we should not disregard late-night eats - in light of the fact that no night out in Sayulita is finished without a quick bite. Luckily, Sayulita's roads are fixed with taco stands and road food sellers presenting flavorful tidbits and late-night chomps to fulfil your desires following an evening of moving and celebration.

Traditional Mexican Cuisine

Sayulita is a food sweetheart's heaven, offering a tempting exhibit of conventional Mexican dishes that feature the country's different culinary legacy. From appetising road tacos to good stews and fiery salsas, Sayulita's cafés and diners present true flavours that will leave you hankering more.

How about we start with breakfast - the main dinner of the day, Mexican-style. Envision yourself sitting at a radiant outside bistro, tasting on a steaming cup of newly blended espresso as you scrutinise the menu. From exemplary dishes like huevos rancheros and chilaquiles to local fortes like machaca con huevo and molletes, Sayulita's morning meal choices are however fluctuated as they may be delectable. Remember to add a side of newly made salsa and a crate of warm tortillas to finish your morning dinner.

For lunch, why not enjoy some customary Mexican road food? Sayulita's roads are fixed with taco stands and food trucks serving delectable dishes like tacos al minister, carnitas, and barbacoa. Pull up a stool, request a plate of your #1 tacos, and tweak them with a variety of garnishes like cilantro, onion, salsa, and lime. Wash everything down with a cold cerveza or agua fresca for the ideal late morning dinner.

As the sun sets, now is the ideal time to test a portion of Sayulita's heartier charge. Going to one of the town's numerous eateries represents considerable authority in provincial food, where you can devour dishes like pozole, mole, and birria. These tasty stews and meals are made with different meats, vegetables, and flavours, bringing about dishes that are rich, consoling, and very fulfilling.

What's more, we should not disregard dessert - in light of the fact that no dinner is finished without something sweet. Sayulita is home to a few bread kitchens and pastry shops presenting tasty deals like churros, flan, and tres leches cake. Indulge yourself with a sweet guilty pleasure and fulfil your sweet tooth prior to going out to investigate Sayulita's dynamic nightlife scene.

Beachfront Restaurants

Sayulita's beautiful shoreline is speckled with beguiling oceanfront cafés and bistros, offering amazing perspectives on the sea and new ocean breezes to go with your feast. Whether you're longing for fish, Mexican works of art, or worldwide passage, feasting at an ocean front eatery in Sayulita is an encounter not to be missed.

Envision finding a spot at a table with your toes in the sand, watching the sun sink underneath the skyline as you taste a revived mixed drink and relish the kinds of Mexico. Numerous ocean front eateries in Sayulita work in new fish dishes like ceviche, barbecued fish, and shrimp tacos, made with privately gotten fixings and presented with a side of sea sees.

Notwithstanding fish, you'll likewise track down different dishes on the menu, including tacos, quesadillas, mixed greens, and that's just the beginning. Whether you're feasting with family, companions, or that unique individual, the casual air and staggering landscape make eating at an ocean front café in Sayulita an essential encounter.

Bars and Nightclubs

As the sun sets and the stars emerge, Sayulita's roads wake up with energy and fervour, offering a lively nightlife scene that is ideally suited for those hoping to move the night away or partake in a couple of beverages with companions. From enthusiastic bars to clamouring clubs, Sayulita has something for everybody with regards to nightlife.

Begin your night with a dusk mixed drink at one of the town's oceanfront bars or housetop lounges. Taste on a margarita or mojito as you watch the sky turn shades of pink and orange, projecting a warm gleam over the sea and the town underneath. It's the ideal method for loosening up and starting off an evening of tomfoolery and merriments.

As the night advances, Sayulita's roads wake up with music, chuckling, and moving. Make a beeline for the town square, known as Court Sayulita, where local people and sightseers the same accumulate to mingle and appreciate unrecorded music and diversion. Sit down on one of the seats or dance under the stars as nearby artists and entertainers make that big appearance.

Assuming that you're in the mood for moving, Sayulita has a few clubs and bars where you can move the night away to the hints of live DJs and groups. From reggae and salsa to electronic and rock, there's no deficiency of music and dance floors to keep you moving until the early hours of the morning.

For a more easygoing night, why not go to one of Sayulita's comfortable wine bars or high quality mezcalerias? Taste on a glass of wine or test a portion of Mexico's best mezcal as you blend with local people and individual explorers, sharing stories and making new companions en route.

Taco Stands and Food Trucks

No visit to Sayulita is finished without inspecting a portion of the town's popular road tacos and food truck passage. Sayulita's roads are fixed with taco stands and food trucks serving up heavenly dishes that are however reasonable as they seem to be delightful.

From tacos al minister to carne asada, carnitas, and that's only the tip of the iceberg, Sayulita's taco stands offer a wide assortment of fillings and fixings to fulfil each hankering. Pick your number one meats, heap on the garnishes like cilantro, onion, salsa, and lime, and partake in your tacos in a hurry or at one of the close by tables.

Notwithstanding tacos, you'll likewise find an assortment of other road food sources at Sayulita's food trucks, including quesadillas, tortas, tamales, and that's only the tip of the iceberg. These portable restaurants are an extraordinary choice for a fast and fulfilling feast on the run, whether you're investigating the town or making a beeline for the ocean side for a day of sun and surf.

Chapter 6: Shopping in Sayulita

Shopping in Sayulita – a bright and lively experience that is as much about investigating the town's enchanting roads and meeting neighbourhood craftsmans for what it's worth tracking down exceptional fortunes to bring back home. As somebody who has meandered through the clamouring markets and store shops of this enchanting Mexican town, let me be your manual for the diverse universe of shopping in Sayulita.

Nearby Markets:

Sayulita is home to a few clamouring markets where you can track down everything from high quality specialties and distinctive products to new delivery and nearby luxuries. One of the most famous business sectors is the Mercado del Pueblo, held each Friday morning in the town square, Court Sayulita. Here, you'll find a beautiful exhibit of slowing down selling hand tailored gems, materials, earthenware, from there, the sky's the limit, all created by neighbourhood craftsmans utilising customary methods that went down through ages. It's the ideal spot to search for exceptional trinkets and gifts to bring back home.

Notwithstanding the Mercado del Pueblo, Sayulita likewise has a week after week ranchers market where you can load up on new foods grown from the ground, high quality cheeses, custom made bread, and other privately created merchandise. Held each Tuesday morning, the ranchers market is an extraordinary spot to test a portion of the district's culinary enjoyments and backing nearby ranchers and makers.

Store Shops:

Sayulita's roads are fixed with enchanting store shops and exhibitions, offering a mother lode of remarkable finds and unique fortunes. Whether you're looking for handcrafted adornments, bohemian attire, or beautiful home stylistic layout, Sayulita's stores have something for everybody.

Meander down Calle Delfines and Calle Revolución, two of the town's principal shopping roads, and you'll find an assortment of store shops selling all that from hand tailored calfskin merchandise and woven materials to mind boggling beaded gems and lively work of art. A significant number of these shops are possessed and worked by nearby craftsmans, offering you the chance to meet the creators and find out about the craftsmanship behind their manifestations.

One of my #1 store in Sayulita is Galeria Tanana, a wonderful exhibition and studio space displaying crafts by nearby craftsmen and craftsmans. Here, you'll track down a staggering assortment of high quality gems, pottery, works of art, and models, all roused by the regular magnificence and dynamic culture of Sayulita and the encompassing district. It's the ideal spot to track down a special piece of craftsmanship or gems to celebrate your time in Sayulita.

Surf Shops:

Sayulita is a surfer's heaven, and no visit to the town would be finished without an outing to one of its many surf shops. Whether you're needing another board, some surf wax, or a snazzy bathing suit, Sayulita's surf shops take care of you.

One of the most well known surf shops in Sayulita is Lunazul Surf School and Shop, found right around the ocean in the core of town. Here, you'll track down a wide determination of surfboards, paddleboards, and other water athletic gear, as well as surf illustrations and rentals for fledglings and experienced riders. The proficient staff are dependably glad to give counsel and suggestions to assist you with finding the ideal stuff for your riding experience.

Another must-visit surf shop in Sayulita is MexiLogFest, a surf shop and exhibition having some expertise in longboard surfing and retro surf culture. Peruse their assortment of rare surfboards, high quality blades, and exemplary surf clothing, or go for a walk through the display to respect crafted by neighbourhood specialists and picture takers enlivened by the surf way of life. A laid-back and varied shop captures the pith of Sayulita's surf culture.

High quality Tequila and Mezcal:

No excursion to Sayulita would be finished without inspecting a portion of Mexico's best tequila and mezcal. Sayulita is home to a few store shops and tasting rooms where you can test and buy an assortment of high quality spirits, including tequila, mezcal, and raicilla, a customary agave soul local to the district.

One of the most outstanding spots to test tequila and mezcal in Sayulita is Raicilla Tasting Room, a comfortable and welcoming space found simply off the town square. Here, you can appreciate direct tastings of an assortment of distinctive spirits, finding out about the creation cycle and tasting the extraordinary flavours and smells of every one. Whether you're a carefully prepared specialist or new to the universe of agave spirits, Raicilla Tasting Room offers a tomfoolery and instructive experience for all.

Beachwear and Souvenirs:

Obviously, no outing to Sayulita would be finished without getting some snazzy beachwear and keepsakes to recall your time in this enchanting Mexican town. Sayulita's roads are fixed with shops selling everything from brilliant sarongs and straw caps to hand tailored shoes and surf-enlivened attire.

Go to Sayulita Beachwear, found right on the fundamental ocean side, for a wide determination of swimwear, ocean side embellishments, and gifts. Here, you'll find all that you want for a day of sun and surf, from beautiful bathing suits and concealments to oceanside towels, sunscreen, and that's only the tip of the iceberg. It's the ideal way to load up on fundamentals prior to raising a ruckus around town.

For one of a kind and hand tailored trinkets, make certain to look at Sayulita's craftsman markets and store shops. Whether you're searching for hand tailored ceramics, beaded gems, or unpredictably woven materials, you're certain to track down something uniquely great to help you to remember your time in Sayulita. Also, remember to wrangle - haggling is important for the shopping experience in Mexico, and you might have the option to score a few extraordinary arrangements on your buys.

Local Artisans and Boutiques

Something I totally adored about Sayulita was its flourishing local area of neighbourhood craftsmans and stores. Meandering through the vivid roads, I coincidentally found a gold mine of handcrafted merchandise and extraordinary tracks down that caught the embodiment of Mexican craftsmanship and inventiveness.

Calle Delfines and Calle Revolución, two of the central avenues in Sayulita, are fixed with store shops displaying craftsmanship by nearby craftsmans. As I wandered through these enchanting roads, I really wanted to be attracted to the lively shows and eye-getting retail facades.

One of my #1 store was Galeria Tanana, a wonderful display and studio space where I found a variety of dazzling high quality gems, ceramics, canvases, and models. Each piece was a show-stopper, enlivened by the normal magnificence and lively culture of Sayulita and the encompassing district. I wound up buying a couple of mind boggling hoops made by a neighbourhood craftsman, a souvenir that I'll esteem long into the future.

Another champion store was Xilotl, a comfortable shop that spent significant time in high quality materials and home stylistic layout. Here, I found a staggering assortment of woven covers, weaved pad covers, and vivid embroidered works of art, all made with adoration and care by nearby craftsmen utilising customary strategies that went down through ages. I was unable to oppose getting a couple of parts to add a dash of Mexican style to my home.

Souvenir Shops

No outing to Sayulita would be finished without getting a couple of keepsakes to recollect my time in this energetic Mexican town. Luckily, Sayulita is home to an assortment of trinket shops and stores where I tracked down a lot of one of a kind and paramount souvenirs to bring back with me.

Sayulita Beachwear, found right on the fundamental ocean side, was one of my number one spots to search for trinkets. Here, I tracked down a wide determination of beachwear, embellishments, and keepsakes, including bright sarongs, straw caps, and surf-roused clothing. I got a Sayulita shirt and a high quality arm band as a sign of my time in this beguiling ocean side town.

Another extraordinary keepsake shop was Sayulita Sol Gems, a store spend significant time in hand tailored gems enlivened by the excellence of Sayulita and the encompassing locale. I was unable to oppose perusing their assortment of beaded wristbands, turquoise neckbands, and silver hoops, each piece a wearable show-stopper that encapsulated Sayulita's bohemian energy.

Markets and Street Vendors

Sayulita's business sectors and road merchants are a gala for the faculties, offering a dynamic and energetic shopping experience that is not to be missed. From clamoring markets to brilliant road slows down, there's something for everybody to find and investigate.

One of the features of my outing was visiting the Mercado del Pueblo, held each Friday morning in the town square, Court Sayulita. Here, I found an exuberant and clamoring market loaded up with slows down selling all that from new produce and custom made prepared products to handcrafted creates and high quality merchandise. I went through hours meandering through the market, examining heavenly tidbits, talking with nearby sellers, and getting novel keepsakes to bring back home with me.

Notwithstanding the Mercado del Pueblo, Sayulita likewise has a week by week ranchers market where I tracked down different privately created merchandise, including natural leafy foods, high quality cheeses, and custom made jelly. It was the ideal put to load up on new fixings and backing neighbourhood ranchers and makers.

Obviously, no visit to Sayulita would be finished without inspecting a portion of the heavenly road food presented by the town's sellers. From tacos and tamales to elote and churros, Sayulita's roads are fixed with food slows down serving up delectable bites and treats. I was unable to oppose enjoying a couple of tacos al minister and a reviving agua fresca as I investigated the clamouring roads of Sayulita.

Chapter 7: Day Trips and Excursions

Sayulita might be an unassuming community, however its area on the Riviera Nayarit makes it the ideal base for investigating the magnificence and variety of the encompassing region. From perfect seashores and segregated islands to lavish wildernesses and enchanting provincial towns, there are vast open doors for road trips and journeys simply ready to be found.

Marietas Islands:

One of the most famous road trips from Sayulita is a visit to the Marietas Islands, a dazzling archipelago found simply off the coast. Known for their stunning excellence and plentiful marine life, the islands are a shelter for swimmers, jumpers, and nature darlings the same.

I left on a boat visit from Sayulita, cruising across the shimmering waters of the Pacific Sea to arrive at the Marietas Islands. As we moved toward the islands, I was awestruck by their tough excellence - transcending precipices, stowed caverns, and perfect seashores extending as should have been obvious.

Our most memorable stop was Playa del Love, otherwise called the Secret Oceanside, an isolated bay secret inside a characteristic stone development. We wore our swimming stuff and swam through a thin passage to arrive at the ocean side, where we were welcomed by perfectly clear waters and delicate white sand. It was like venturing into a secret heaven, encompassed by the magnificence of nature.

Subsequent to investigating Playa del Love, we proceeded with our boat visit around the islands, halting at different swimming spots to swim among vivid coral reefs and exotic fish. We saw dolphins playing in the waves, ocean turtles floating smoothly through the water, and, surprisingly, a manta beam taking off underneath us. It was a remarkable encounter, submerging ourselves in the regular marvels of the sea.

San Pancho:

For a sample of valid Mexican appeal, I chose to require a road trip to San Pancho, a beguiling beach front town found simply a short drive from Sayulita. Known for its easy going air and immaculate sea shores, San Pancho offers a brief look into conventional Mexican life away from the vacationer swarms.

I leased a vehicle and drove along the grand waterfront parkway, going through rich wildernesses and beautiful towns while heading to San Pancho. As I showed up in the neighbourhood, I was struck by its curious appeal - cobblestone roads fixed with brilliant houses, vivacious courts loaded up with local people, and a casual energy that appeared to penetrate the air.

I went through the day investigating San Pancho's lovely sea shores, relaxing in the sun, and swimming in the warm waters of the Pacific Sea. I likewise meandered through the town's craftsman markets and store shops, getting high quality gifts and visiting with nearby craftsmans about their art.

For lunch, I ate at a neighbourhood fish eatery disregarding the ocean side, enjoying new ceviche, barbecued fish, and super cold cervezas. It was the ideal method for refuelling and loosening up prior to proceeding with my investigation of this beguiling waterfront town.

Sayulita Jungle:

While Sayulita is known for its wonderful sea shores, it's likewise encircled by rich wildernesses and tropical woodlands simply ready to be investigated. One of my number one roadtrips was a wilderness travelling experience through the Sayulita Wilderness, where I found secret cascades, secret swimming openings, and stunning perspectives on the encompassing scene.

I joined a direct visit driven by an educated nearby aide who took us outside of what might be expected and into the core of the wilderness. As we climbed through thick vegetation and transcending trees, we experienced extraordinary untamed life like bright birds, butterflies, and, surprisingly, an intermittent monkey swinging through the shade above.

Our most memorable stop was a secret cascade concealed in the wilderness, where we took a reviving plunge in the cool, completely clear waters. It was an enchanted encounter, encompassed by the sights and hints of nature as we swam underneath the flowing cascade.

Subsequent to chilling at the cascade, we proceeded with our climb through the wilderness, following restricted trails and crossing chattering streams until we arrived at a disconnected swimming opening somewhere down in the backwoods. Here, we took one more dunk in the reviving waters, encompassed by the tranquil excellence of the wilderness.

As we advanced back to Sayulita, I couldn't resist the opportunity to feel a feeling of appreciation for the potential chance to investigate such a delightful and various scene. From the unblemished seashores of the Marietas Islands to the enchanting roads of San Pancho and the lavish wildernesses encompassing Sayulita, every road trip offered its own remarkable experience and left me with recollections that I'll esteem for a lifetime.

Marietas Islands

The Marietas Islands - an unlikely treasure simply off the shore of Sayulita that won my love with its stunning excellence and wealth of marine life. Leaving on a boat visit from Sayulita, I set off to investigate this unblemished archipelago, anxious to find its secret fortunes.

As our boat travelled across the perfectly clear waters of the Pacific Sea, I couldn't resist the opportunity to be hypnotised by the staggering landscape unfurling before me. Transcending bluffs rose from the ocean, their rough edges cut by hundreds of years of wind and waves, while stowed away caverns tempted to be investigated.

Our most memorable stop was Playa del Love, otherwise called the Secret Oceanside, a separated bay settled inside a characteristic stone development. To arrive at this secret heaven, we needed to swim through a thin passage that opened up into a sun-soaked ocean side encompassed by transcending bluffs. It was like venturing into a mysterious world, distant from the rushing about of regular day to day existence.

In the wake of investigating Playa del Love, we proceeded with our boat visit around the islands, halting at different swimming spots to wonder about the energetic coral reefs and vivid fish that called these waters home. We saw dolphins playing in the waves, ocean turtles skimming nimbly through the water, and, surprisingly, a manta beam taking off underneath us. It was a submerged wonderland, overflowing with life and excellence every step of the way.

As we advanced back to Sayulita, I couldn't resist the opportunity to feel thankful for the chance to encounter the normal marvels of the Marietas Islands. From the secret sea shores and secret caverns to the plentiful marine life and unblemished waters, it was a day I will always remember.

San Pancho

Simply a short drive from Sayulita lies the enchanting waterfront town of San Pancho, an unexpected, yet invaluable treasure that won my love with its easygoing energy and bona fide Mexican appeal. I went through a day investigating this pleasant town, meandering through its cobblestone roads and absorbing its casual air.

As I showed up in San Pancho, I was quickly struck by its curious excellence - beautiful houses decorated with bougainvillaea, exuberant courts loaded up with local people, and a feeling of serenity that appeared to pervade the air. It was the ideal break from the hurrying around of city life, offering a brief look into customary Mexican culture and lifestyle.

I went through the day investigating San Pancho's lovely sea shores, relaxing in the sun, and swimming in the warm waters of the Pacific Sea. Playa San Pancho, the town's primary oceanside, was a completely flawless heaven, with delicate brilliant sand and clear blue waters extending as should have been obvious. I went through hours absorbing the sun, paying attention to the waves, and watching the world go by.

Notwithstanding its delightful sea shores, San Pancho is likewise home to a lively expressions and culture scene. I meandered through the town's craftsman markets and store shops, appreciating the high quality gems, materials, and work of art in plain view. I likewise visited the EntreAmigos public venue, a neighbourhood charitable association devoted to advancing training, maintainability, and imagination locally. Here, I had the amazing chance to find out about the middle's different projects and drives, from reusing and natural preservation to craftsmanship and professional preparation.

For lunch, I feasted at a neighbourhood fish café disregarding the ocean side, enjoying new ceviche, barbecued fish, and super cold cervezas. It was the ideal method for refuelling and loosening up prior to proceeding with my investigation of this enchanting waterfront town.

As the sun set, I hesitantly bid goodbye to San Pancho, realising that I would convey its excellence and serenity with me long after I left. It was a day loaded up with remarkable minutes and esteemed recollections, and one that I'll cherish long into the future.

Punta Mita

Settled on a pleasant landmass simply a short drive from Sayulita, Punta Mita is a sumptuous hotel town that offers a sample of heaven with its immaculate sea shores, top notch fairways, and selective conveniences. I went through a day investigating this upscale territory, absorbing the sun, and enjoying the better things throughout everyday life.

As I showed up in Punta Mita, I was promptly struck by its magnificence - lavish tropical nurseries, shining vastness pools, and clearing perspectives on the Pacific Sea extending as should have been obvious. It was a world away from the clamouring roads of Sayulita, offering a feeling of extravagance and quietness that was difficult to stand up to.

I went through the day relaxing by the pool at one of Punta Mita's selective oceanside clubs, tasting on mixed drinks and absorbing the sun. The help was faultless, with mindful staff taking care of my every need and guaranteeing that I had all that I wanted for a day of unwinding and extravagance.

Notwithstanding its lovely sea shores and sumptuous conveniences, Punta Mita is likewise home to the absolute best fairways in Mexico. I played a round at the Jack

Nicklaus-planned Pacifico Fairway, where I was blessed to receive dazzling sea sees and testing openings that tested my abilities. It was a paramount encounter, starting against the background of the Pacific Sea and feeling the warm sea breeze on my skin.

For lunch, I ate at one of Punta Mita's connoisseur eateries, enjoying new fish, barbecued meats, and scrumptious mixed drinks. The food was a-list, with flavours that moved on my sense of taste and left me hankering more. It was a culinary experience that surpassed my assumptions and left me feeling fulfilled and content.

As the day approached, I hesitantly bid goodbye to Punta Mita, realising that I would convey its magnificence and extravagance with me long after I left. It was a day loaded up with extravagance and unwinding, and one that I'll esteem long into the future.

Puerto Vallarta

As I started my day in Puerto Vallarta, I chose to begin with a comfortable walk around the notorious Malecón, the clamouring promenade that stretches along the city's pleasant waterfront. Fixed with palm trees, models, and road entertainers, the Malecón is the ideal spot to absorb the lively climate of Puerto Vallarta.

As I strolled along the Malecón, I really wanted to be enraptured by the staggering perspectives on the shining Pacific Sea on one side and the vivid structures of the memorable downtown area on the other. I stopped to respect the great figures that spot the promenade, including the famous "Los Arcos" design, an image of Puerto Vallarta's rich social legacy.

Subsequent to investigating the Malecón, I advanced into the core of Puerto Vallarta's noteworthy Old Town, referred to locally as "Zona Romántica." Here, slender cobblestone roads are fixed with enchanting bistros, store shops, and craftsmanship displays, making a lively and mixed climate that is ideal for investigating.

One of the features of my visit to Old Town was the Congregation of Our Woman of Guadalupe, a dazzling church building that rules the horizon with its chime tower and multifaceted design. I ventured inside to respect the elaborate inside, with its brilliant stained glass windows and delightfully embellished raised areas, prior to lighting a candle and offering a request for harmony and flourishing.

Subsequent to investigating Old Town, I chose to wander further inland to investigate the lavish wildernesses and mountains that encompass Puerto Vallarta. I left on a direct climbing visit through the Sierra Madre mountains, where I found secret cascades, beautiful waterways, and stunning vistas of the encompassing scene.

One of the features of the climb was a visit to a customary Mexican town, where I had the chance to meet neighbourhood craftsmans, find out about conventional specialties like ceramics and winding around, and test delightful natively constructed cooking made with new, privately obtained fixings. It was an interesting look into country Mexican life and an indication of the rich social legacy that lies just past the clamouring roads of Puerto Vallarta.

As the sun set, I advanced back to Malecón to get the nightfall over the Pacific Sea. I found a spot on the oceanfront and watched in wonderment as the sky detonated in an uproar of varieties, painting the mists with shades of pink, orange, and purple. It was an otherworldly second that helped me to remember the magnificence and miracle of Puerto Vallarta, a city that had caught my heart with its dynamic culture, shocking view, and warm friendliness.

Chapter 8: Itineraries for Different Travellers

Whether you're an ocean side darling, an experienced searcher, a foodie, or a culture lover, Sayulita brings something to the table for each sort of voyager. As somebody who has investigated this dynamic Mexican town, I'm eager to share a few point by point schedules custom fitted to various interests and inclinations. How about we make a plunge!

Ocean side Darling's Paradise:

For the people who can't get enough of sun, sand, and ocean, Sayulita is the ideal objective. Begin your day with a comfortable walk around the immaculate shores of Sayulita Ocean side, where you can absorb the sun, take a reviving dunk in the turquoise waters, and watch surfers ride the waves.

In the wake of burning some major calories, make a beeline for one of the ocean front eateries covering the shore for a delectable fish lunch with a view. Attempt new ceviche, barbecued fish tacos, or a tropical natural product smoothie while relaxing in an ocean side seat with your toes in the sand.

In the early evening, investigate a portion of Sayulita's other wonderful sea shores, for example, Playa de los Muertos or Playa Carricitos, both simply a short walk or drive away. These disconnected spots offer a more serene and confined environment, ideal for sunbathing, swimming, and partaking in the normal excellence of the shoreline.

As the sun sets, advance back to Sayulita Ocean side to get the stunning nightfall over the sea. Get a virus drink from one of the ocean side bars and watch as the bay windows up in a kaleidoscope of varieties, projecting a brilliant shine over the water. It's the ideal finish to a day in heaven.

Experience Searcher's Dream:

For those hankering fervour and adrenaline-syphoning exercises, Sayulita offers a lot of chances for experience. Begin your day with an exhilarating zip line visit through the lavish wildernesses encompassing the town, taking off high over the treetops and getting a charge out of stunning perspectives on the scene underneath.

A while later, go to the Sayulita Wilderness for a directed climbing journey, where you can investigate stowed cascades, swim in confined swimming openings, and experience extraordinary natural life like monkeys, birds, and butterflies. It's an extraordinary method for drenching yourself in nature and experiencing the magnificence of the Mexican wilderness very close.

In the early evening, hit the waves and take a shot at surfing or stand-up paddleboarding, two of Sayulita's most well known water sports. Whether you're a novice or an accomplished rider, there are a lot of surf schools and rental shops around where you can prepare and stir things up around town.

As the sun sets, trade your surfboard for a trail blazing bicycle and leave on an exhilarating downhill ride through the tough landscape encompassing Sayulita. Feel the surge of adrenaline as you explore winding paths, rough ways, and steep drops, all while getting a charge out of all encompassing perspectives on the sea and shoreline beneath. It's an undertaking you will probably remember forever.

Foodie's Delight:

For voyagers who love to eat and drink their direction through an objective, Sayulita is a culinary heaven. Begin your day with a visit to the Sayulita Ranchers Market, held each Tuesday morning in the town square, Court

Sayulita. Here, you can test different neighbourhood rarities, including new foods grown from the ground, distinctive cheeses, custom made bread, and that's only the tip of the iceberg.

In the wake of perusing the market, make a beeline for one of Sayulita's numerous bistros for a comfortable breakfast or early lunch. Attempt a conventional Mexican breakfast of chilaquiles or huevos rancheros, matched with a newly fermented cup of privately obtained espresso or an invigorating agua fresca.

In the early evening, leave on a culinary visit through Sayulita's best diners, testing various dishes and flavours from road tacos and fish ceviche to connoisseur combination cooking and customary Mexican top picks. Make certain to save space for dessert – Sayulita is home to a few delectable sweet treats, including handcrafted frozen yoghurt, churros, and cakes.

As the night draws near, go to one of Sayulita's oceanfront eateries for a heartfelt supper with a view. Watch the nightfall over the sea as you enjoy new fish, barbecued meats, and scrumptious mixed drinks, all while absorbing the casual climate and warm neighbourliness of Sayulita's feasting scene.

Culture Aficionado's Journey:

For explorers keen on history, craftsmanship, and culture, Sayulita offers a lot of chances to submerge yourself in the nearby legacy and customs. Begin your day with a visit to the Sayulita Workmanship Walk, held each Friday night in the town place. Here, you can investigate exhibitions and studios displaying crafts by nearby craftsmen and craftsmans, from artworks and models to earthenware production and materials.

After the craftsmanship walk, make a beeline for the Sayulita Social Place for a sample of customary Mexican culture and diversion. Appreciate unrecorded music, dance exhibitions, and theatre creations, or partake in studios and classes zeroed in on customary specialties like stoneware, winding around, and cooking.

In the early evening, take a direct visit through Sayulita's noteworthy tourist spots and attractions, including the Congregation of Our Woman of Guadalupe, the town's focal square, and the beautiful roads of Old Town. Find out about the set of experiences and meaning of these destinations from educated neighbourhood guides, and gain a more profound comprehension of Sayulita's rich social legacy.

As the day draws near, join a customary Mexican party or celebration, where you can celebrate with local people and experience the dynamic music, dance, and cooking of Mexico. Whether it's a strict parade, a social festival, or a road party, Sayulita's celebrations offer a remarkable chance to interface with the neighbourhood local area and drench yourself in the soul of Mexico.

Family-Friendly Itinerary

As an investigated parent Sayulita with my family, I comprehend the significance of finding exercises and encounters that are pleasant for the two grown-ups and youngsters the same. Sayulita is the ideal objective for families, offering a great many family-accommodating attractions and exercises that make certain to make enduring recollections. Here is an itemised schedule for an exciting family get-away in Sayulita:

Day 1: Appearance and Ocean side Day

Begin your family get-away in Sayulita with a loosening up day at the ocean side. Sayulita Ocean side is ideal for families, with its delicate waves, delicate sand, and dynamic environment. Go through the day building sandcastles, playing in the surf, and absorbing the sun. Make certain to pack a lot of sunscreen, bites, and water to keep everybody agreeable and hydrated over the course of the day.

For lunch, make a beeline for one of the ocean front cafés or nibble stands coating the shore for an easygoing feast with a view. Attempt conventional Mexican dishes like fish tacos, quesadillas, or ceviche, which are all certain to kindly even the pickiest eaters in the family.

In the early evening, have some time off from the sun and investigate the town of Sayulita. Meander through the beautiful roads, peruse the stores and keepsake shops, and test some scrumptious frozen yoghourt or new natural product from one of the road sellers. Look out for the notorious brilliant paintings and road workmanship that embellish the walls of structures all through the town - they create incredible photographs of open doors!

Day 2: Family Experience Day

Today, leave on a family experience to investigate the regular magnificence and natural life of Sayulita. Begin your day with a directed nature climb through the lavish wilderness encompassing the town. Your aide will lead you through winding paths, calling attention to local plants and creatures en route. Watch out for monkeys, birds, and butterflies – no one can really tell what you could experience!

After your climb, cool off with a visit to a nearby cascade. Many visit administrators offer directed excursions to stowed cascades where you can swim in the reviving waters and partake in a cookout lunch in the shade. It's an incredible method for encountering the excellence of Sayulita's normal scene and making remarkable recollections with your loved ones.

In the early evening, make a beeline for one of Sayulita close by attractions for more family fun. Visit the Vallarta Greenhouses to investigate the different vegetation of the locale, or take a boat visit to the Marietas Islands to snorkel, swim, and investigate stowed away seashores and caverns. Anything you pick, there's no deficiency of experience to be had in Sayulita!

Day 3: Social Investigation and Relaxation

Today, enjoy some time off from experience and go through the day submerging yourselves in the rich culture and history of Sayulita. Begin your day with a visit to the Sayulita Social Center, where you can find out about customary Mexican specialties, music, and dance. Partake in a studio or class to take a shot at ceramics, winding around, or cooking - it's a tomfoolery and instructive experience for the entire family.

A short time later, visit the Congregation of Our Woman of Guadalupe, a delightful house of prayer situated in the core of Sayulita's memorable Old Town. Respect the staggering engineering and brilliant stained glass windows, and pause for a minute to reflect and value the excellence of the congregation's inside.

In the early evening, make a beeline for one of Sayulita close by sea shores for some unwinding and free time. Playa Los Muertos and Playa Carricitos are both incredible choices for families, with their quiet waters and tranquil environment. Bring along a cookout lunch and go through the early evening time relaxing in the sun, building sandcastles, and sprinkling in the waves.

Day 4: Sayulita Market and Departure

On your last day in Sayulita, make certain to visit the Sayulita Ranchers Market, held each Tuesday morning in the town square, Court Sayulita. Here, you can pursue slowing down selling new produce, hand tailored artworks, and scrumptious bites and treats. Get a few gifts to bring back home with you and appreciate one final taste of Sayulita's lively culture and local area.

After the market, invest your excess energy in Sayulita absorbing the last piece of sun and surf around the ocean. Take one last plunge in the sea, gather shells along the shore, and relish the experiences of unwinding and fellowship with your loved ones.

Adventure Seekers Itinerary

Hello there, thrill seekers! Assuming you're like me and flourish with energy and rush looking for exercises, Sayulita is the ideal objective for your next experience. From surfing and zip-covering to wilderness journeys and swimming, this lively Mexican town has everything. Here is a point by point schedule for an activity pressed experience searchers' excursion in Sayulita:

Day 1: Surf's Up!

Prepare to raise a ruckus around town and experience the excitement of surfing in Sayulita, one of Mexico's chief riding objections. Begin your day as early as possible with a surf example from one of the neighbourhood surf schools. They'll give all the stuff you really want and master guidance to assist you with getting your most memorable wave - regardless of whether you're a complete fledgling as was I!

After your surf example, use whatever remains of the day rehearsing your recently discovered abilities on Sayulita Ocean side. With its delicate waves and sandy base, Sayulita Ocean side is ideal for amateurs and experienced surfers. Snatch a board and oar out, feeling the surge of adrenaline as you ride the waves and absorb the sun.

Day 2: Zip-covering and Wilderness Trekking

Today, now is the ideal time to take your experience higher than ever with an exhilarating zip-lining visit through the rich wildernesses encompassing Sayulita. Lash in and take off through the treetops, getting a charge out of all encompassing perspectives on the wilderness covering underneath and the shimmering Pacific Sea somewhere far off. It's an encounter you will probably remember forever!

After your zip-lining experience, proceed with your excursion through the wilderness with a directed travelling visit. Follow twisting paths through thick vegetation, crossing streams and spotting extraordinary untamed life en route. Your aide will lead you to stowed away cascades and mystery swimming openings, where you can chill with a reviving dunk in the completely clear waters. It's a wilderness experience straight out of a film!

Day 3: Swimming and Island Hopping

Today, investigate the submerged marvels of the Pacific Sea with a swimming and island-jumping journey to the Marietas Islands. Board a boat and journey across the turquoise waters, respecting the dazzling landscape of the islands as you go. Watch out for dolphins, ocean turtles, and even whales assuming that you're fortunate!

Showing up at the Marietas Islands, wear your swimming stuff and plunge into the perfectly clear waters to investigate energetic coral reefs abounding with exotic fish. Swim through submerged caverns and passages, wondering about the magnificence of this safeguarded marine safe-haven. Remember to watch out for the renowned "Stowed away Ocean side," an isolated inlet concealed inside a characteristic stone development – it's an unquestionable requirement!

Day 4: Mountain Trekking and Dusk Hike

On your last day of experience in Sayulita, get your heart syphoning with a mountain trekking trip through the rough landscape encompassing the town. Lease a bicycle and hit the paths, exploring rough ways, steep plunges, and twisting bends as you investigate the picturesque open country.

Feel the surge of adrenaline as you race down the mountainside, getting a charge out of stunning perspectives on the sea and shoreline beneath.

As the sun sets, ribbon up your climbing boots and set out on a dusk climb to Monkey Mountain, perhaps of Sayulita's most famous milestone. Follow the path to the highest point, where you'll be compensated with all encompassing perspectives on the encompassing scene washed in brilliant light. It's the ideal method for finishing your experience-filled get-away in Sayulita, absorbing the excellence of nature and thinking about the unbelievable encounters you've had en route.

Relaxation Retreat Itinerary

Good day, individual unwinding searchers! Assuming you're needing a few rest and revival, Sayulita is the ideal objective for your next escape. With its easygoing energy, flawless sea shores, and quiet environment, this beguiling Mexican town is a definitive unwinding retreat. Here is an itemised schedule for a tranquil excursion in Sayulita:

Day 1: Appearance and Ocean side Day

Begin your unwinding retreat in Sayulita with a relaxed day at the ocean side. Sayulita Ocean side is the ideal spot to loosen up, with its delicate sand, delicate waves, and dazzling sea sees. Go through the day relaxing in the sun, paying attention to the waves, and partaking in the serene air. Make certain to pack a decent book, an ocean side towel, and a lot of sunscreen to keep you agreeable over the course of the day.

For lunch, make a beeline for one of the ocean front eateries or tidbit stands coating the shore for a heavenly feast with a view. Attempt conventional Mexican dishes like fish tacos, ceviche, or aguachile, all made with new, privately obtained fixings. Wash it down with a reviving agua fresca or a cold cerveza - you're an extended get-away, all things considered!

Day 2: Yoga and Wellness

Today, now is the right time to feed your body, psyche, and soul with a day of yoga and wellbeing exercises. Begin your morning with a reviving yoga class at one of Sayulita's numerous yoga studios or ocean front retreats. Whether you're a carefully prepared yogi or a fledgling, there's a class for each level and capacity.

After your yoga meeting, indulge yourself with a loosening up spa treatment or back rub to mitigate tired muscles and liquefy away any waiting pressure or strain. Sayulita is home to various spas and health focuses offering a scope of all encompassing treatments and medicines, from conventional

Mexican temazcal functions to lavish back rubs and facials.

Day 3: Ocean front Bliss

Go through another joyful day absorbing the sun and surf in Sayulita's lovely sea shores. Pack a cookout lunch and make a beeline for one of the town's more separated sea shores, for example, Playa de los Muertos or Playa Carricitos, for a serene day of unwinding and isolation. Bring along a decent book, an ocean side umbrella, and a lot of sunscreen, and go through the day relaxing in the shade, paying attention to the waves, and partaking in the regular excellence of the shore.

In the early evening, go for a comfortable walk along the ocean side or investigate the tide pools and rock developments that dab the coastline. Watch out for bright shells, crabs, and other marine life - no one can really tell what treasures you could find!

Day 4: Dusk Sail and Goodbye Fiesta

On your last day in Sayulita, indulge yourself with a mystical nightfall sail along the coast. Board a sailboat or boat and set forth as the sun plunges underneath the skyline, projecting a brilliant gleam over the sea. Taste on a glass of champagne or a tropical mixed drink as you journey along the shore, watching the sky wake up with dynamic tones.

Chapter 9: COVID-19 Considerations

In these exceptional times, focusing on wellbeing and security while travelling is fundamental. As somebody who has investigated Sayulita during the Coronavirus pandemic, I grasp the significance of avoiding potential risk to safeguard yourself as well as other people. Here are a few critical contemplations to remember while visiting Sayulita:

Remain Informed: Prior to heading out to Sayulita, remain informed about the most recent Coronavirus rules and guidelines given by neighbourhood specialists and wellbeing associations. Monitor any tourism warnings or limitations that might influence your excursion, and be ready to in like manner change your arrangements.

Practise Social Distancing: While investigating Sayulita, be aware of social separating rules and stay away from swarmed places whenever the situation allows. Keep a separation of something like six feet from others, particularly in occupied regions like business sectors, cafés, and sea shores.

Wear a Mask: As per neighbourhood guidelines, wear a veil or mask in broad daylight spaces, indoor settings, and whatever other regions where social separation might challenge. Ensure your veil covers your nose and mouth safely and supplant it assuming that it becomes clammy or dirtied.

Wash Your Hands: Practise great hand cleanliness by cleaning up every now and again with cleanser and water for somewhere around 20 seconds, particularly in the wake of contacting surfaces or items in open regions. In the event that cleanser and water are not accessible, use hand sanitizer with somewhere around 60% liquor.

Stay away from High-Hazard Activities: Consider keeping away from high-risk exercises and encounters that might expand your possibilities of openness to Coronavirus, like swarmed parties, enormous social events, or close-physical games. Settle on outside exercises and outdoors settings whenever the situation allows.

Get Vaccinated: Assuming you're qualified, consider receiving any available immunisation shots against Coronavirus prior to making a trip to Sayulita. Immunisation can fundamentally decrease your gamble of extreme ailment and transmission of the infection, assisting with safeguarding yourself as well as other people locally.

Be Respectful: Regard the wellbeing and security estimates executed by neighbourhood organisations, lodgings, and attractions in Sayulita. Adhere to any posted signage or guidelines with respect as far as possible, guest plans, and other Coronavirus conventions.

Screen Your Health: Stay watchful and screen your wellbeing for any side effects of Coronavirus during your time in Sayulita. On the off chance that you experience side effects like fever, hack, or trouble breathing, look for clinical consideration right away and heed the guidance of medical care experts.

Support Neighbourhood Businesses: Show your help for the nearby local area in Sayulita by disparaging private ventures, cafés, and craftsmans who might have been affected by the pandemic. Your help can assist with animating the nearby economy and safeguard the remarkable culture and appeal of Sayulita.

Travel Restrictions and Requirements

Prior to setting out on your excursion to Sayulita, it's significant to remain refreshed on the most recent travel limitations and prerequisites forced by both your nation of origin and Mexico. These actions can change contingent upon the ongoing Coronavirus circumstance and unofficial laws. Here are a few central issues to consider:

Entry Requirements: Mexico has carried out passage prerequisites for voyagers showing up via air, including finishing a wellbeing statement structure and going through wellbeing screenings upon appearance. A few carriers may likewise require evidence of a negative Coronavirus test taken inside a certain time period before flight.

Travel Insurance: Consider buying travel protection that incorporates inclusion for Coronavirus related costs, for example, clinical treatment and quarantine costs. This can give genuine serenity and monetary assurance if there should be an occurrence of surprising conditions during your outing.

Quarantine Protocols: Know about any quarantine conventions that might be set up upon appearance in Mexico. While isolation prerequisites might differ depending upon your nation of beginning and immunisation status, it's fundamental to consent to neighbourhood guidelines to forestall the spread of the infection.

Border Restrictions: Check for any boundary limitations or terminations that might affect your itinerary items, including land line intersections among Mexico and adjoining nations. Remember that line approaches can change quickly in light of advancing Coronavirus advancements.

Vaccination Requirements: Stay informed about any immunisation prerequisites or suggestions for voyagers to Mexico. While inoculation isn't presently required for section into the nation, being completely immunised can give an additional layer of insurance against Coronavirus.

Health and Safety Measures

Guaranteeing your wellbeing and security while making a trip to Sayulita includes following thorough wellbeing and wellbeing estimates executed by nearby specialists and organisations. Here are a few fundamental precautionary measures to remember:

Mask-Wearing: Wear a veil or mask as per nearby guidelines, particularly in indoor public spaces, swarmed regions, and while social separation is beyond the realm of possibilities. Convey additional veils with you and guarantee they cover your nose and mouth appropriately.

Hand Hygiene: Practise regular hand cleanliness by cleaning up with cleanser and water for somewhere around 20 seconds or utilising hand sanitizer with no less than 60% liquor content. Regularly practise it to clean your hands when contacting surfaces or articles in open regions.

Physical Distancing: Keep a protected separation of no less than six feet from others, especially in jam-packed places like business sectors, eateries, and public transportation. Keep away from close contact with people who are not a part of your movement gathering to limit the gamble of transmission.

Sanitization Practices: Go to proactive lengths to clean regularly contacted surfaces, for example, entryway handles, handrails, and electronic gadgets, utilising sanitizer wipes or splashes. Consider conveying a movement estimated container of hand sanitizer for disinfection in a hurry.

Avoiding Crowds: Limit your openness to swarmed settings and enormous social occasions to diminish the gamble of Coronavirus transmission. Settle on outside exercises and outdoors attractions where ventilation is better and physical removal can be kept up with all the more successfully.

Responsible Travel Practices

Dependable travel rehearses assume an essential part in safeguarding the wellbeing and prosperity of neighbourhood networks and saving the common habitat. Here are a few ways to rehearse capable travel in Sayulita:

Respect Neighborhood Regulations: Get to know nearby guidelines and rules connected with Coronavirus, as well as social standards and customs in Sayulita. Regard any limitations or prerequisites forced by specialists and conform to them as needs be.

Support Nearby Businesses: Show your help for neighbourhood organisations, craftsmans, and business visionaries by belittling their foundations and buying privately made items and gifts. Your spending adds to the neighbourhood economy and supports vocations inside the local area.

Minimise Ecological Impact: Do whatever it takes to limit your natural effect while going in Sayulita, like lessening waste, moderating water and energy, and regarding regular environments and untamed life. Discard rubbish mindfully and reuse whenever the situation allows.

Cultural Sensitivity: Be socially touchy and aware towards the neighbourhood populace, customs, and customs in Sayulita. Find out about the social legacy of the district and draw in with local people in a deferential and obliging way.

Leave No Trace: Follow the standards of "Leave No Follow" by leaving regular regions and attractions as you tracked them down, without upsetting the climate or abandoning any litter or waste. Leave just impressions and take just recollections with you.

Chapter 10: What to Do and Not to Do in Sayulita

As somebody who has investigated the enchanting roads and lovely seashores of Sayulita, Mexico, I'm eager to share some insider tips on what to do and what not to do during your visit. Sayulita is a supernatural objective with a dynamic culture, tasty food, and vast open doors for experience. In this way, how about we jump into the rules and regulations to capitalise on your Sayulita experience:

Do's:

Explore the Beaches: Sayulita is known for its shocking sea shores, so make certain to invest a lot of energy absorbing the sun and surf. Whether you're into swimming, sunbathing, or surfing, there's an ocean side for everybody. Try not to miss Sayulita Ocean side for its energetic climate and delicate waves, or dare to calmer spots like Playa de los Muertos for a more loosened up vibe.

Try Nearby Cuisine: One of the features of visiting Sayulita is enjoying the delectable neighbourhood cooking. From delectable tacos and new fish to true Mexican dishes like pozole and mole, there's no deficiency of culinary pleasures to test. Make certain to attempt road food from merchants for a bona fide taste of Mexico, and remember to wash it down with a reviving agua fresca or a cold cerveza.

Embrace the Culture: Sayulita is a dynamic town with a rich social legacy, so carve out an opportunity to drench yourself in the nearby culture. Investigate the beautiful roads fixed with paintings and road craftsmanship, visit the town square (Court Sayulita) to absorb the exuberant air, and don't botch the chance to go to comprehensive developments and celebrations assuming they're occurring during your visit.

Stay Active: With its beautiful scenes and regular excellence, Sayulita offers vast open doors for outside exercises and experiences. Whether you're into surfing, climbing, zip-coating, or horseback riding, there's something for each open air aficionado. Exploit the shocking landscape and get out there to investigate!

Support Nearby Businesses: Sayulita is home to numerous capable craftsmans, independent ventures, and business visionaries, so make certain to help them during your visit. Look for hand tailored specialties, trinkets, and privately made items at the business sectors and shops, feast at family-possessed eateries, and book visits and exercises with neighbourhood administrators to add to the nearby economy and local area.

Don'ts:

Don't Neglect Sun Protection: Sayulita is honoured with bountiful daylight, so make certain to shield yourself from the sun's beams. Remember to load sunscreen with a high SPF, shades, a wide-overflowed cap, and lightweight dress to protect yourself from the sun and forestall sun related burns and intensity depletion.

Don't Litter: Sayulita is a perfect heaven, so make certain to regard the climate by discarding your waste appropriately. Try not to litter on the seashores of roads, and consistently utilise assigned garbage cans to discard squander. Keep in mind, abandoning only impressions is fundamental to protecting the excellence of Sayulita for people in the future to appreciate.

Don't Be Disrespectful: Sayulita is an inviting and comprehensive local area, so make certain to recognize local people and their traditions. Try not to be troublesome or impolite, and consistently request authorization prior to taking photographs of individuals or their property. Keep in mind, you're a visitor in their home, so treat them with benevolence and thought.

Don't Drink Tap Water: While Sayulita has numerous fabulous cafés and diners, being careful about the water is fundamental. Try not to drink faucet water or use it to clean your teeth, as it may not be ok for utilisation. Stick to filtered water or sanitised water from confided in sources to remain hydrated and try not to become ill.

Don't Overindulge: Sayulita is known for its enthusiastic nightlife scene, however it's fundamental to capably appreciate it. Try not to revel in liquor or take part in unsafe ways of behaving, particularly assuming you're out late around evening time. Make sure to take on a steady speed, remain hydrated, and consistently have an arrangement for returning to your facilities securely.

Respect for Local Customs

While visiting Sayulita, Mexico, recognizing the neighbourhood customs and customs of this energetic community is fundamental. As somebody who has invested energy submerging myself in the way of life of Sayulita, I've taken in a couple of things about how to explore consciously through this wonderful town. Here is an itemised guide on regarding neighbourhood customs in Sayulita:

Greetings and Interactions: In Sayulita, good tidings are a fundamental piece of social connection. While meeting somebody interestingly, welcoming them with a well disposed "Hola" or "Buenos días/tardes/noches" (great morning/evening/evening is standard).""
Warmly greet individuals you meet, and remember to visually connect and grin - it's an honourable gesture and kind disposition.

Dress Code: While Sayulita has a laid-back air, it's crucial for dressing unassumingly and consciously, particularly while visiting strict locales or going to far-reaching developments. Abstain from wearing revealing apparel or beachwear openly, and settle on lightweight, breathable textures that cover your shoulders and knees.

Respect for Elders: In Mexican culture, regard for older folks is profoundly esteemed. While interfacing with more seasoned individuals from the local area, utilise formal titles, for example, "Señor" (Mr.) or "Señora" (Mrs.) trailed by their last name as a worthy gesture. Listen mindfully when they talk and try not to hinder or go against them.

Eating and Drinking Etiquette: While feasting in Sayulita, it's standard to trust that everybody at the table will be served prior to starting your dinner. Keep your hands noticeable on the table and try not to lay your elbows on it while eating. Say "¡Buen provecho!" (partake in your dinner) before you begin eating, and consistently finish your plate to show appreciation for the food.

Celebrations and Festivals: Sayulita is known for its brilliant celebrations and festivities consistently. On the off chance that you're sufficiently fortunate to go to one of these occasions, recognize neighbourhood customs and customs by partaking in the celebrations with excitement and a receptive outlook. Be deferential of holy customs and functions and adhere to any rules or guidelines given by occasion coordinators.

Environmental Conservation

Sayulita's normal excellence is quite possibly its most valuable resource, and it's vital to do whatever it takes to secure and save the climate during your visit. Here are a few ways to rehearse natural protection in Sayulita:

Reduce, Reuse, Recycle: Sayulita has restricted squandering the executives foundation, so it's urgent to limit your natural impression by lessening waste whenever the situation allows. Bring reusable water bottles, shopping packs, and utensils to keep away from single-use plastics, and discard rubbish capably in assigned containers.

Conserve Water: Water is a valuable asset in Sayulita, particularly during the dry season. Clean up, switch off taps when not being used, and report any holes or plumbing issues to your facilities. Think about taking part in local area endeavours to moderate water, for example, ocean side cleanups or reforestation projects.

Respect Marine Life: Sayulita is home to different marine life, including ocean turtles, dolphins, and exotic fish. Practise capable swimming and plunging by trying not to contact or upset coral reefs and marine creatures. Pick eco-accommodating visit administrators that focus on manageability and protection endeavours.

Stay on Checked Trails: While climbing or investigating nature trails in Sayulita, stick to stamped ways and trails to limit harm to vegetation and untamed life environments. Abstain from stomping on delicate biological systems or wandering off-trail, as this can prompt disintegration and interruption of normal living spaces.

Support Economical Tourism: Pick facilities, visit administrators, and organisations that focus on reasonable practices and ecological stewardship. Search for eco-accommodating confirmations or drives, like reusing programs, energy-proficient lighting, and water-saving measures, while making travel game plans.

Scams and Tourist Traps to Avoid

While Sayulita is for the most part a protected and inviting objective, similar to any vacationer area of interest, it's fundamental to be watchful and mindful of likely tricks and scams. Here are a few normal tricks to look out for and tips on the most proficient method to keep away from them:

Overcharging: Be careful about sellers or cab drivers who attempt to cheat vacationers for labour and products. Continuously request costs forthright and arrange if important. Look at costs at different foundations prior to making a buy to guarantee you're getting a fair arrangement.

Timeshare Presentations: Whenever drew closer by somebody offering unconditional gifts or limits in return for going to a condo show, tread carefully. These introductions can be high-pressure deals strategies, and you might wind up feeling committed to buy a condo you don't need or need.

Fake Police Officers: In uncommon cases, sightseers have revealed experiences with people acting like cops who endeavour to coerce cash or assets. Whenever drew nearer by somebody professing to be a cop, request to see their ID and identification. On the off chance that you're uncertain, look for help from a formally dressed cop or contact the neighbourhood specialists.

Street Scams: Be careful with road tricks like interruption methods or pickpocketing in packed regions. Keep your assets secure and be wary when drawn closer by outsiders offering spontaneous help or headings. Pay attention to your gut feelings and try not to draw in with dubious people.

Unlicensed Visit Operators: Prior to booking visits or journeys, research the organisation and guarantee they are authorised and legitimate. Unlicensed administrators may not comply with security principles or guidelines, jeopardising your wellbeing. Pick visit administrators with positive audits and proposals from confided in sources.

Conclusion

Indeed, individual voyager, our excursion through Sayulita, Mexico, has reached a conclusion, however the recollections we've made will endure forever. As I consider my time spent in this enchanting seaside town, I can't resist the urge to feel appreciative for the extraordinary encounters, warm cordiality, and energetic culture that characterise Sayulita.

From the second I showed up in Sayulita, I was dazzled by its easy going environment, beautiful roads, and shocking regular excellence. Whether walking around the cobblestone roads fixed with lively paintings or absorbing the sun on the immaculate sea shores, Sayulita has an approach to charming your entire being all along.

One of the features of my visit to Sayulita was encountering the glow and neighbourliness of the nearby local area. From the lively good tidings of the road merchants to the veritable grins of the occupants, I felt wholeheartedly greeted any place I went. The feeling of local area and kinship in Sayulita is really exceptional and causes this town to feel like a usual hangout spot.

Obviously, no visit to Sayulita would be finished without enjoying the scrumptious food that the town brings to the table. From enjoying newly got fish at ocean front eateries to inspecting credible road tacos from nearby merchants, each feast was a culinary pleasure. The kinds of Mexico woke up with each nibble, leaving me hankering all the more lengthy after my excursion had finished.

Be that as it may, past the delightful food and pleasant scenes, Sayulita additionally showed me important illustrations regard, preservation, and capable travel. I figured out how to embrace the nearby traditions and customs, recognizing the way of life and legacy of this dynamic local area. I saw firsthand the significance of ecological preservation, from safeguarding marine life to protecting regular natural surroundings for people in the future to appreciate.

During my time in Sayulita, I additionally turned out to be more cautious and mindful of possible tricks and scams, figuring out how to explore the clamouring roads with certainty and wariness. By remaining educated and alert, I had the option to partake in my movements securely and dependably, without succumbing to normal traps that can once in a while discolour the traveller experience.

As I bid goodbye to Sayulita, I convey with me a gold mine of recollections - from the stunning nightfalls over the Pacific Sea to the enthusiastic parties loaded up with music and dance. Yet, more than that, I convey with me a newly discovered appreciation for the magnificence of Mexico, the glow of its kin, and the sorcery of movement.

Thus, to anybody considering an outing to Sayulita, I say this: go with an open heart, a brave soul, and a readiness to embrace the unexplored world. Permit yourself to become mixed up in the beautiful roads, to appreciate the kinds of nearby food, and to associate with the lively local area that calls Sayulita home. Or more all, make sure to travel dependably, regarding the way of life, climate, and individuals who make Sayulita the enchanted objective that it is.

Once more with respect to me, I realise that Sayulita will constantly hold an extraordinary spot in my heart, and I anticipate the day when I can get back to loll in its magnificence and absorb its perpetual appeal. Up to that point, I convey the soul of Sayulita with me any place I go, a sign of the mind boggling experiences that anticipate the people who try to investigate this charming corner of the world.

Made in the USA
Columbia, SC
17 December 2024